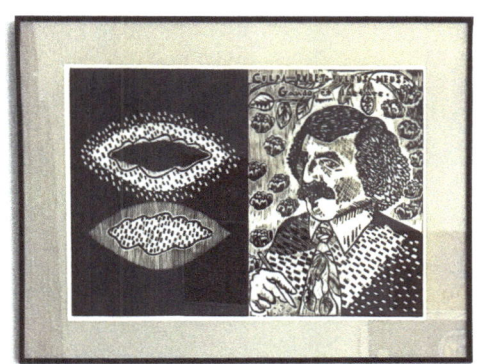

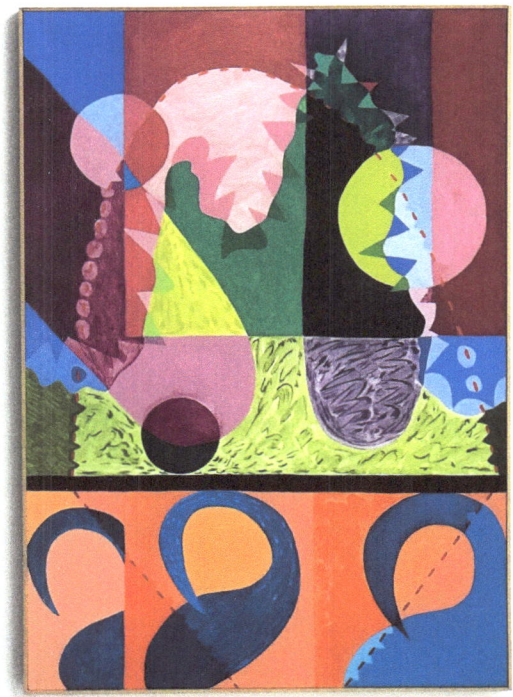

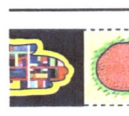

David and Beatrice: Hands and Other Symbols

The Work of David W. Cummings and Beatrice M. Mady
3/13/20 - 5/3/20

Curated by Anne Trauben

VICTORY HALL PRESS

Drawing Rooms celebrates the life and work of David W. Cummings, a life lived together with Beatrice M. Mady. Their work is full of shapes and symbols, and their message is in living color.

David came of age as a painter in the mid-late 1960s. After graduating from the Kansas City Art Institute in 1963, he immersed himself in the Bay Area Figurative Painting scene in San Francisco and soaked in the California light. He moved to New York City after receiving his M.F.A. from the University of Nebraska in 1968. A pioneer in the SoHo art scene, he became part of the Third Generation Abstraction Expressionists and spent the 70s painting and exhibiting in New York City and beyond. David's work was featured in a survey of abstract painting, Lyrical Abstraction, that traveled to museums across the country before finally arriving at the Whitney Museum of American Art in New York City.

In 1977, he met Beatrice when he was giving a lecture at Pratt where she was studying for her M.F.A. The two started a relationship as artists and a romance that would span four decades. By the early 1980s, David and Beatrice had married and left their SoHo loft behind, finding a factory building in the Jersey City Heights neighborhood of Jersey City, and converting it into living/studio spaces.

Pioneers in the Jersey City art scene, they were among the early artists who came to Jersey City and formed relationships with many of the artists in the building fondly referred to as "The 111". Beatrice helped build the arts community through her active participation, encouragement and support in Pro Arts; as a Professor and Gallery Director at Saint Peter's University, and, of course, her artwork.

David passed from us suddenly last year, but he left the brilliance of his work for us to keep. We are excited to show so much of his work in this retrospective, and to exhibit them along with Beatrice's works, highlighting the exciting ways these two artists' works developed and interacted with each other.

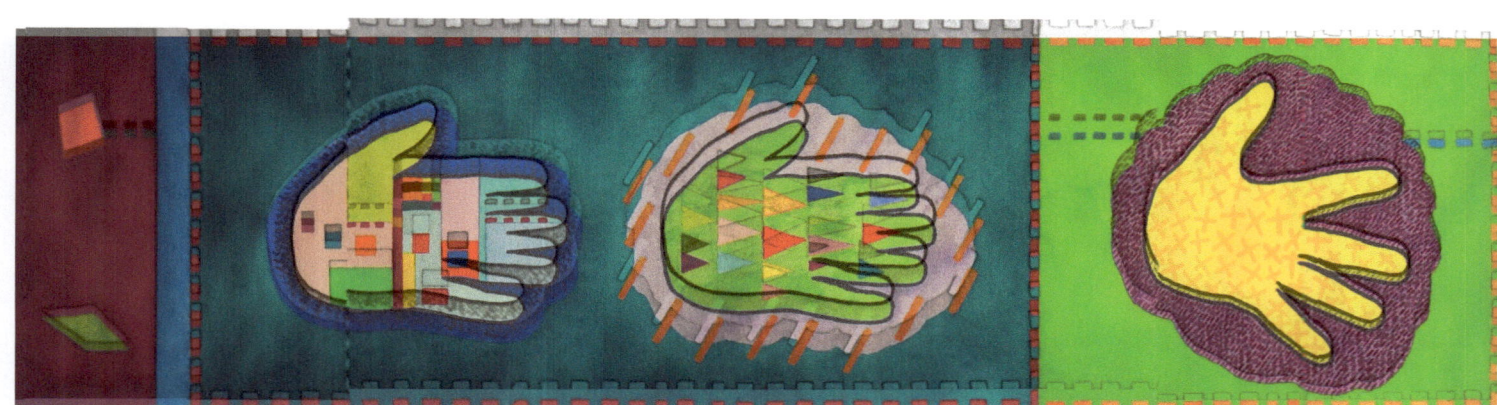

David W. Cummings: Cross Fire, watercolor on paper, 43" x11", 2015

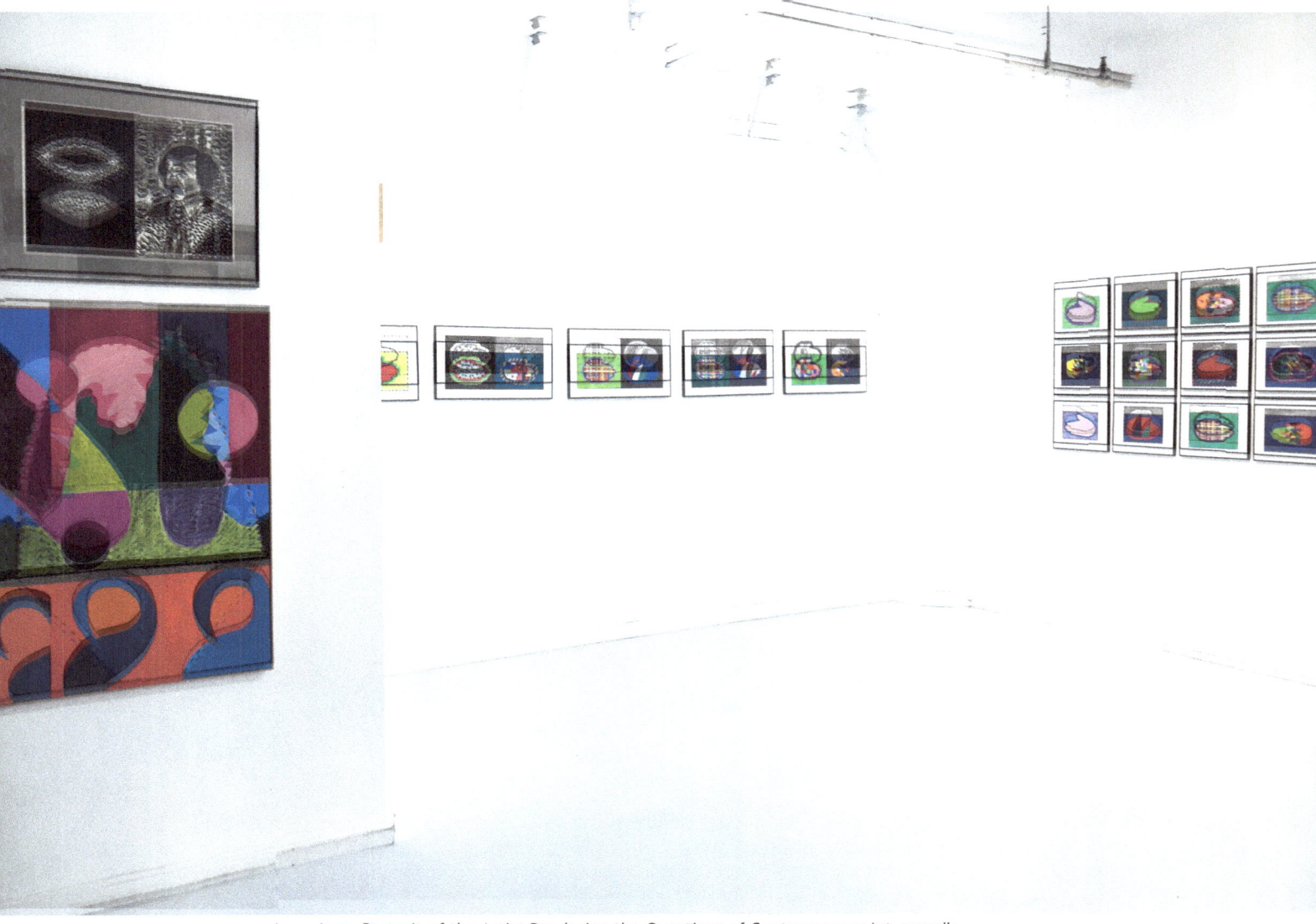

David W. Cummings: Portrait of the Artist Pondering the Questions of Contemporary Art, woodblock print, 23" x 28", 1990
Grid of single hands, watercolor on paper
Double hands, watercolor on paper
Beatrice M. Mady: The Dead Can Dance, oil on canvas, 44" x 30", 1997

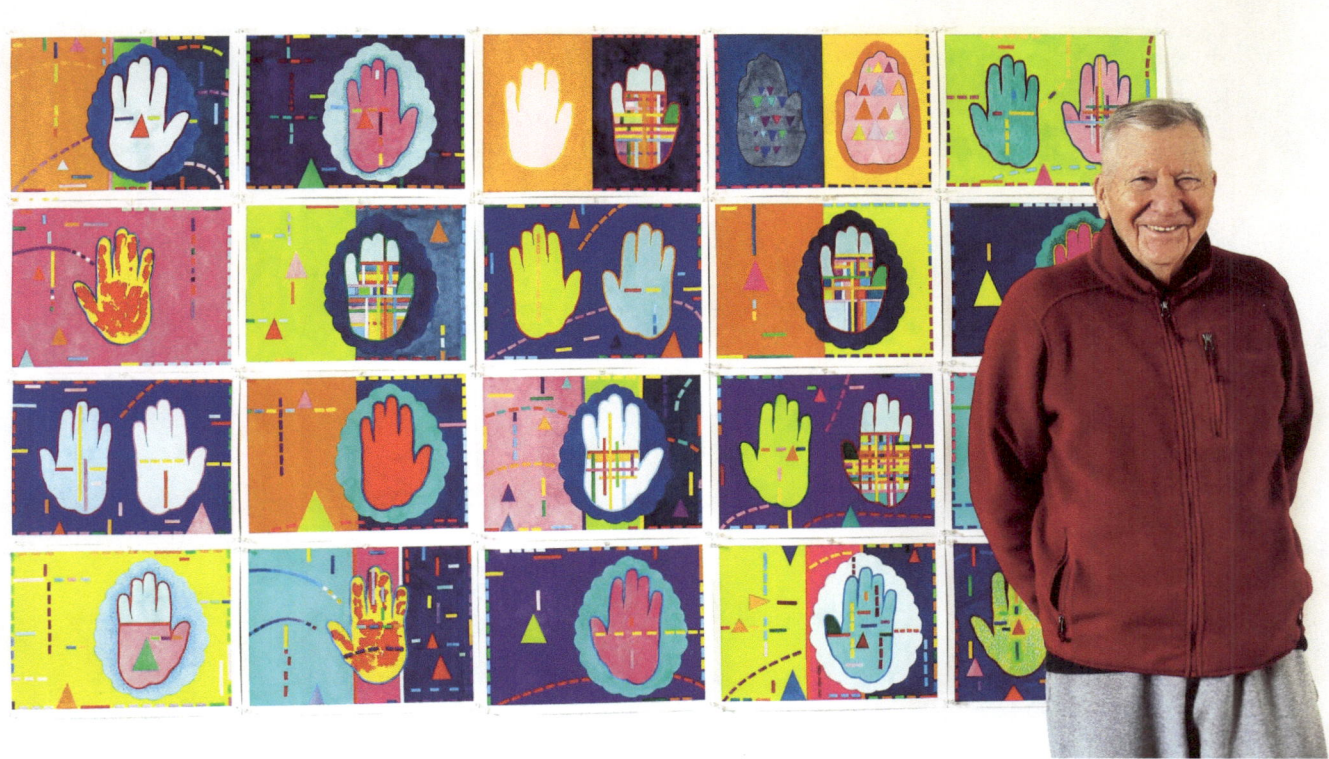

In my current work, I have taken the oldest personal image of the individual human, the hand-print or hand tracing, and attempted to bring it up-to-date as a visual self-portrait of the twenty-first century. This type of documentation has been used and recorded in every known society and is one of the earliest sources of the existence of the human being individually being recorded by the individual human themself. The basic shape(s) that I am using is (are) a tracing of an individual human hand. Mine. Some earlier paintings were taken from a variety of peoples hands including couples in a "His and Hers" series but my current work uses only my own hands in the tradition of the artist "Self Portrait".

After the basic shapes of the piece are determined, I turn to the tool of color, my favorite tool, to produce, define, and interpret the issue of visual expressionism in a modern, art school educated, show biz influenced Paleolithic tradition.

The question is if I can take such an image that has such a long human history, found in kindergarten classroom paintings, used in commercial ads and mass communications, and still transform that image into my very own personal statement of Contemporary High Art.

David W. Cummings, 2019

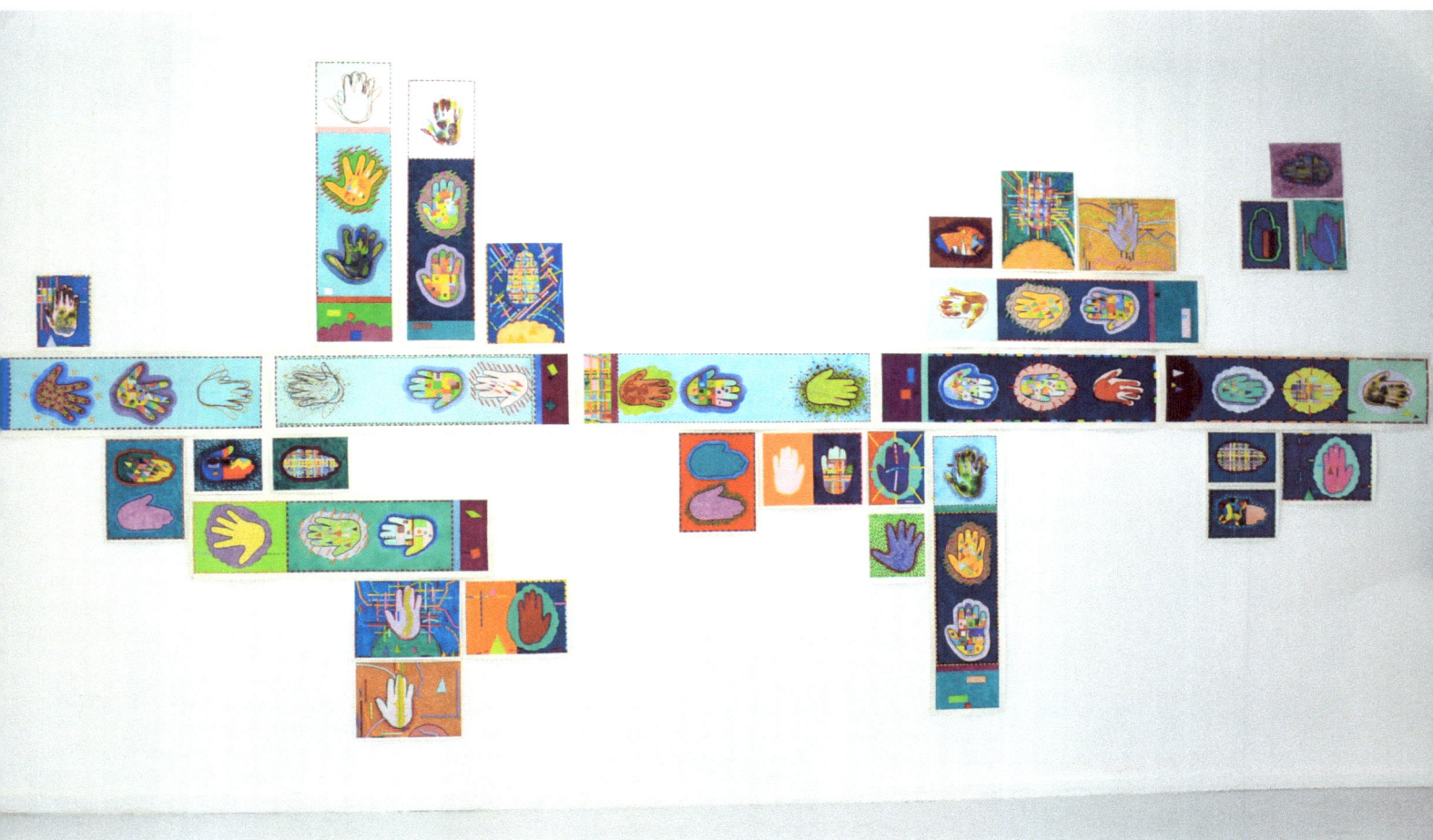

David W. Cummings: Grid of Hands, watercolor on paper

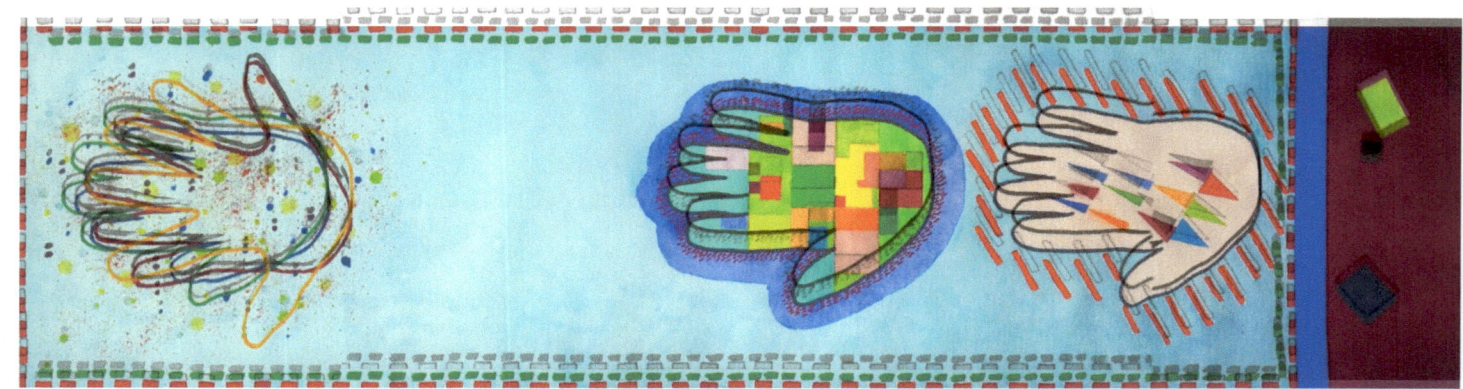

David W. Cummings: He Who Became a God, watercolor on paper, 43" x 11", 2015

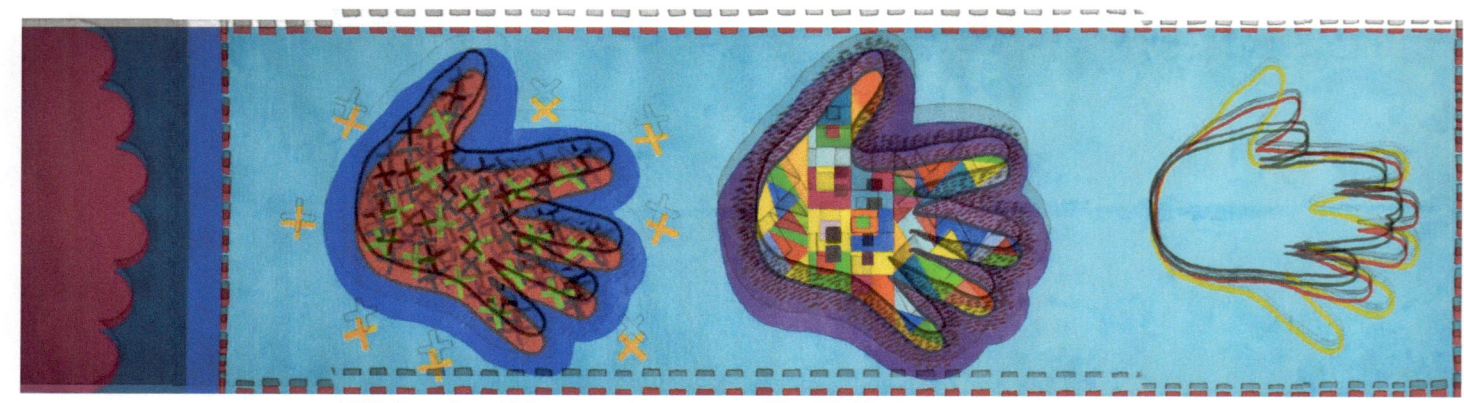

David W. Cummings: Kali, watercolor on paper, 43" x 11", 2014

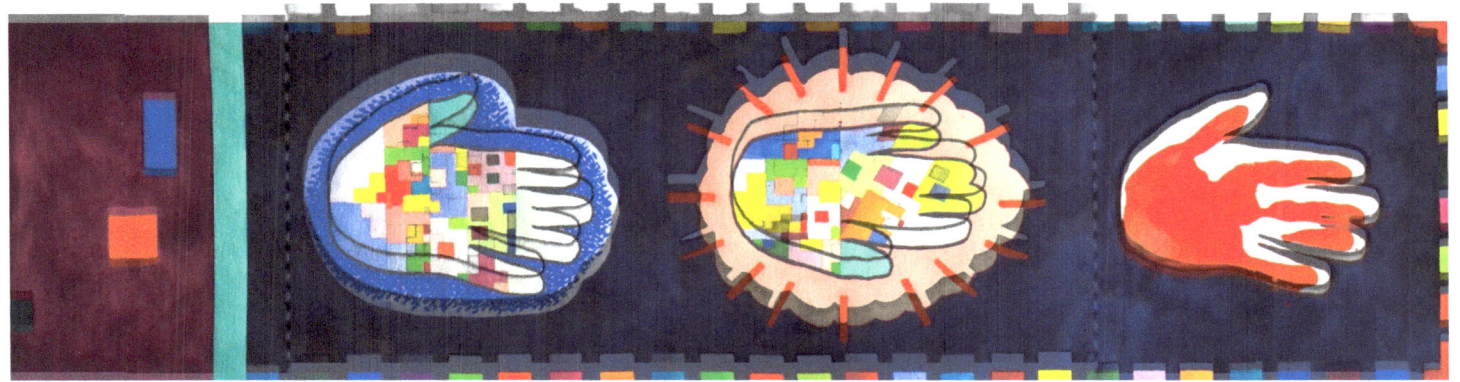

David W. Cummings: Witch Hunter, watercolor on paper, 43" x 11"; 2015

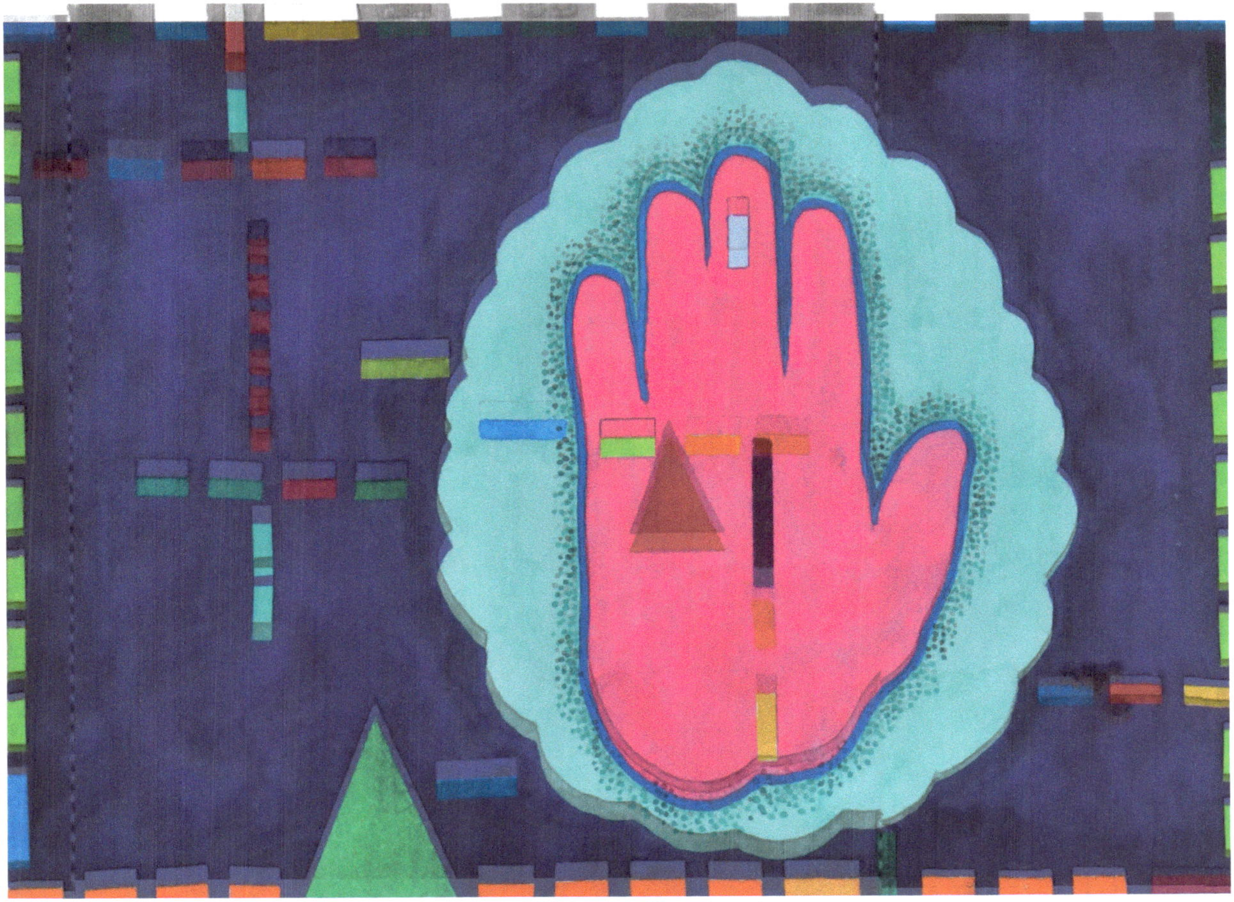

David W. Cummings: Self Portrait #8, watercolor on paper, 11" x 15"; 2017

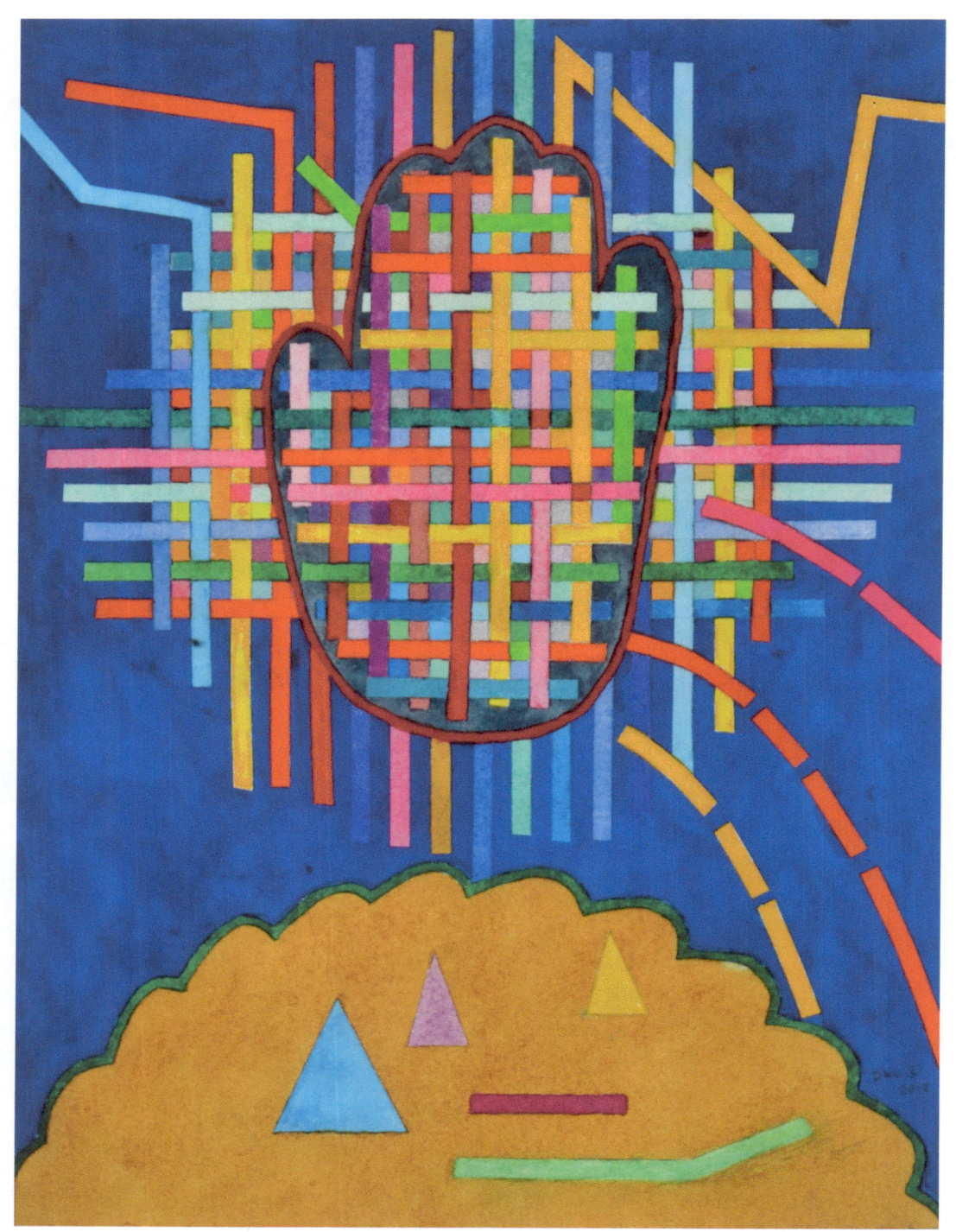

David W. Cummings: Travel Through Time and Space, watercolor on paper, 11" x 15", 2018

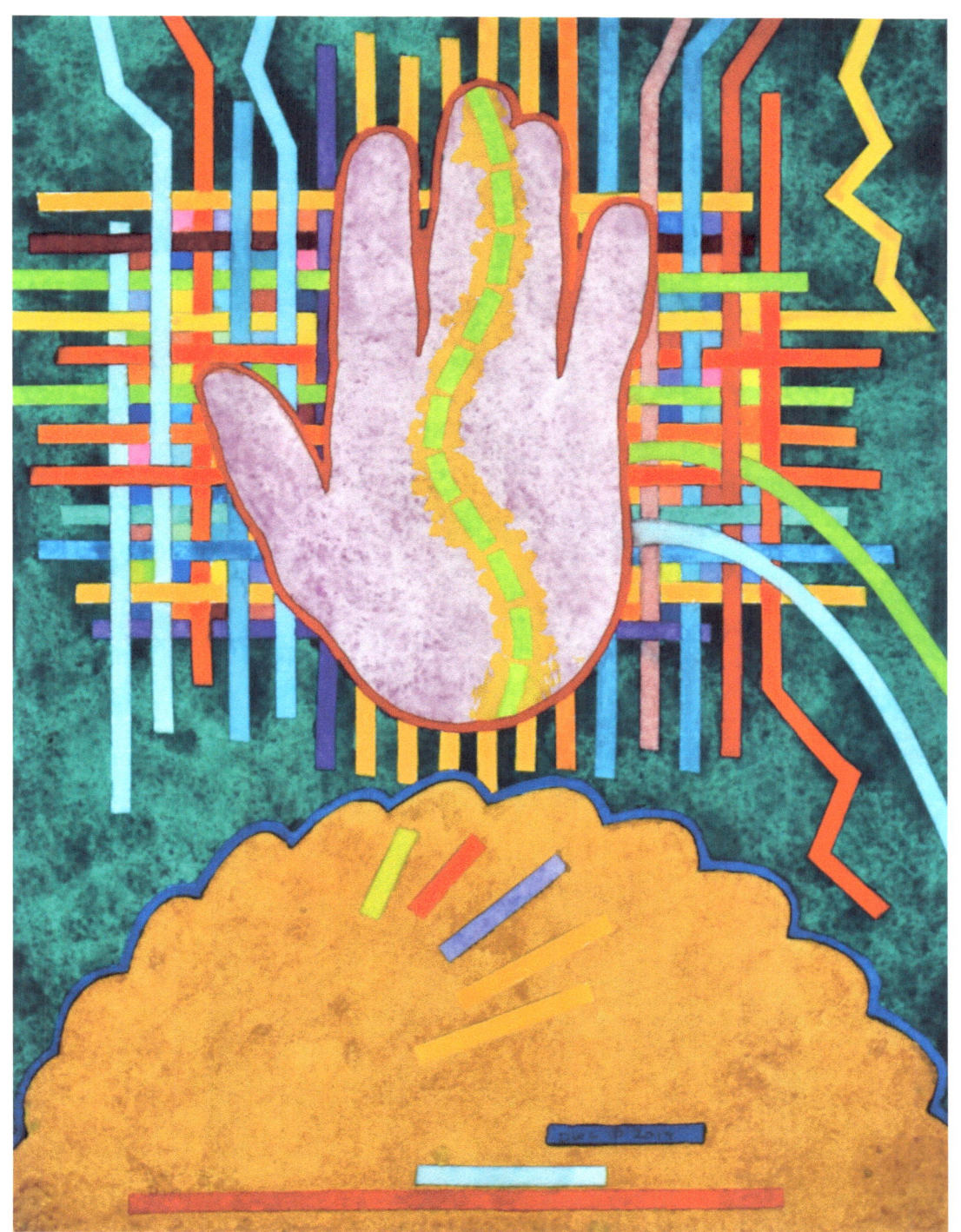
David W. Cummings: On Top, watercolor on paper, 11" x 15 ", 2019

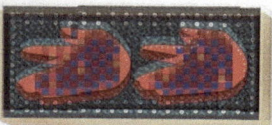 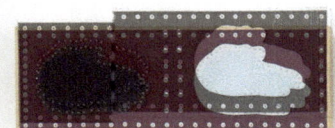 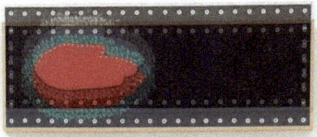 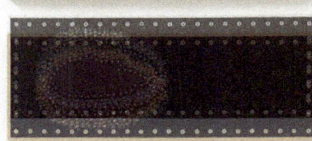 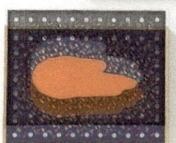  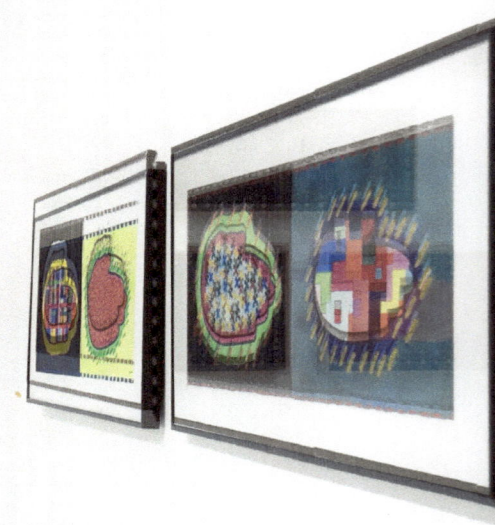

Opposite page top: David W. Cummings, Born in the Dark, oil on panel, 8" x 12", 1996

Bottom: David W. Cummings, The Lonely Foot Soldier, oil on panel, 9" x 12", 1995

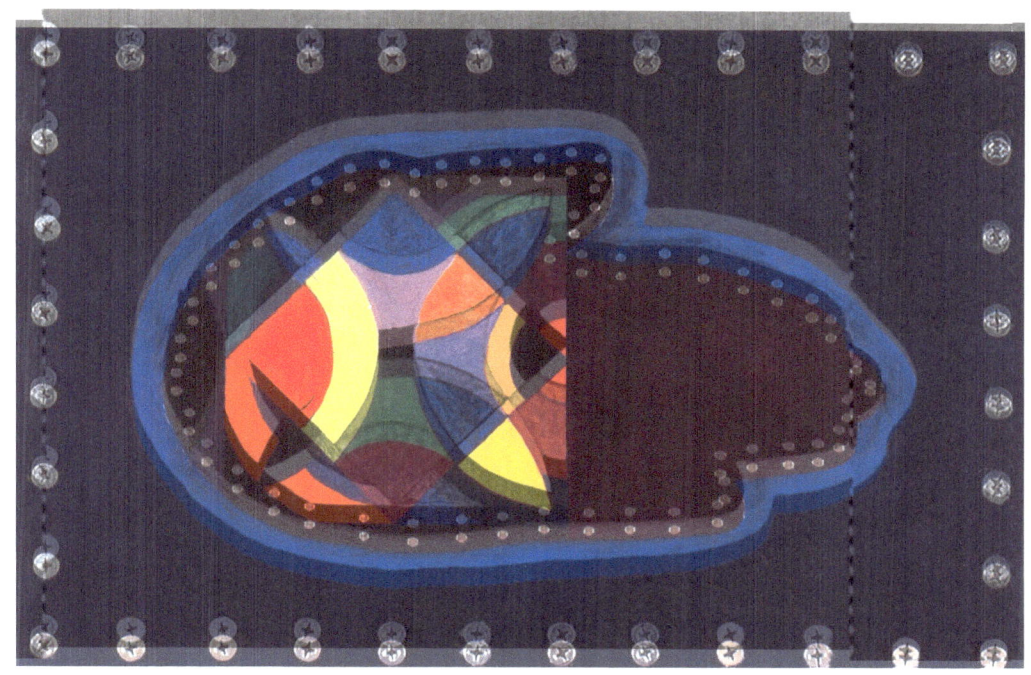
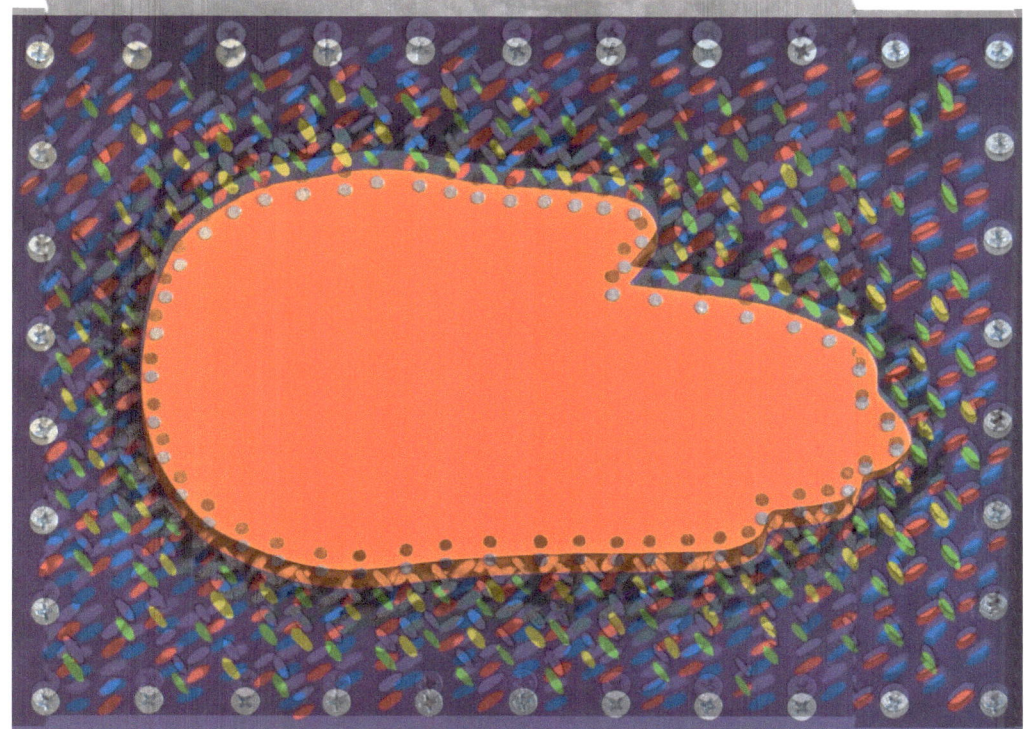

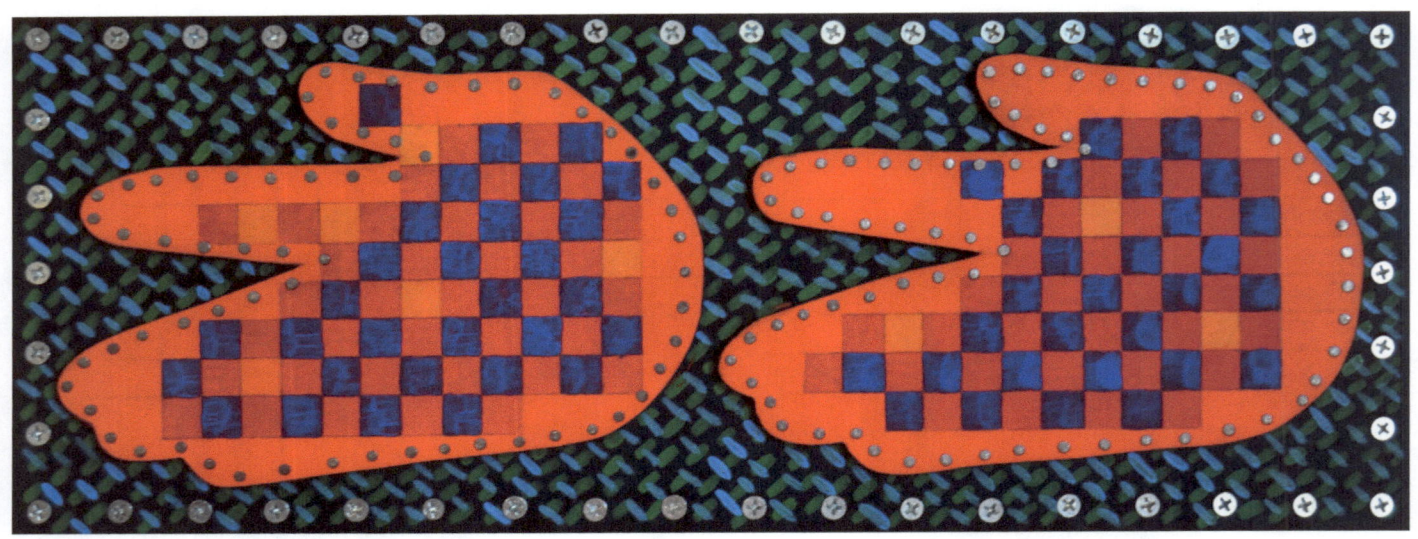

David W. Cummings: Raconteur, oil on panel, 8" x 19", 1997

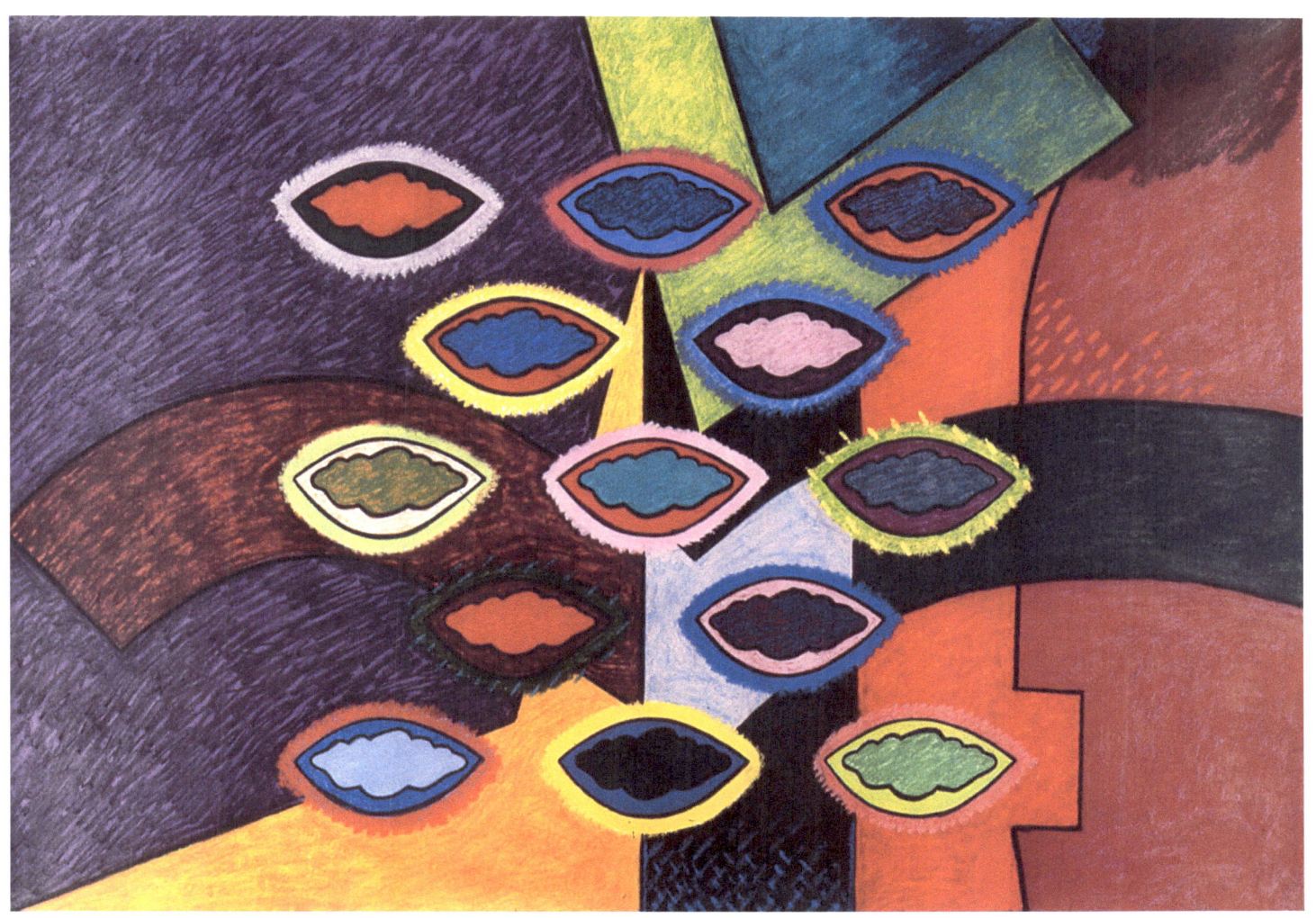

David W. Cummings: Montauk, pastel on paper, 30" x 42", 1993

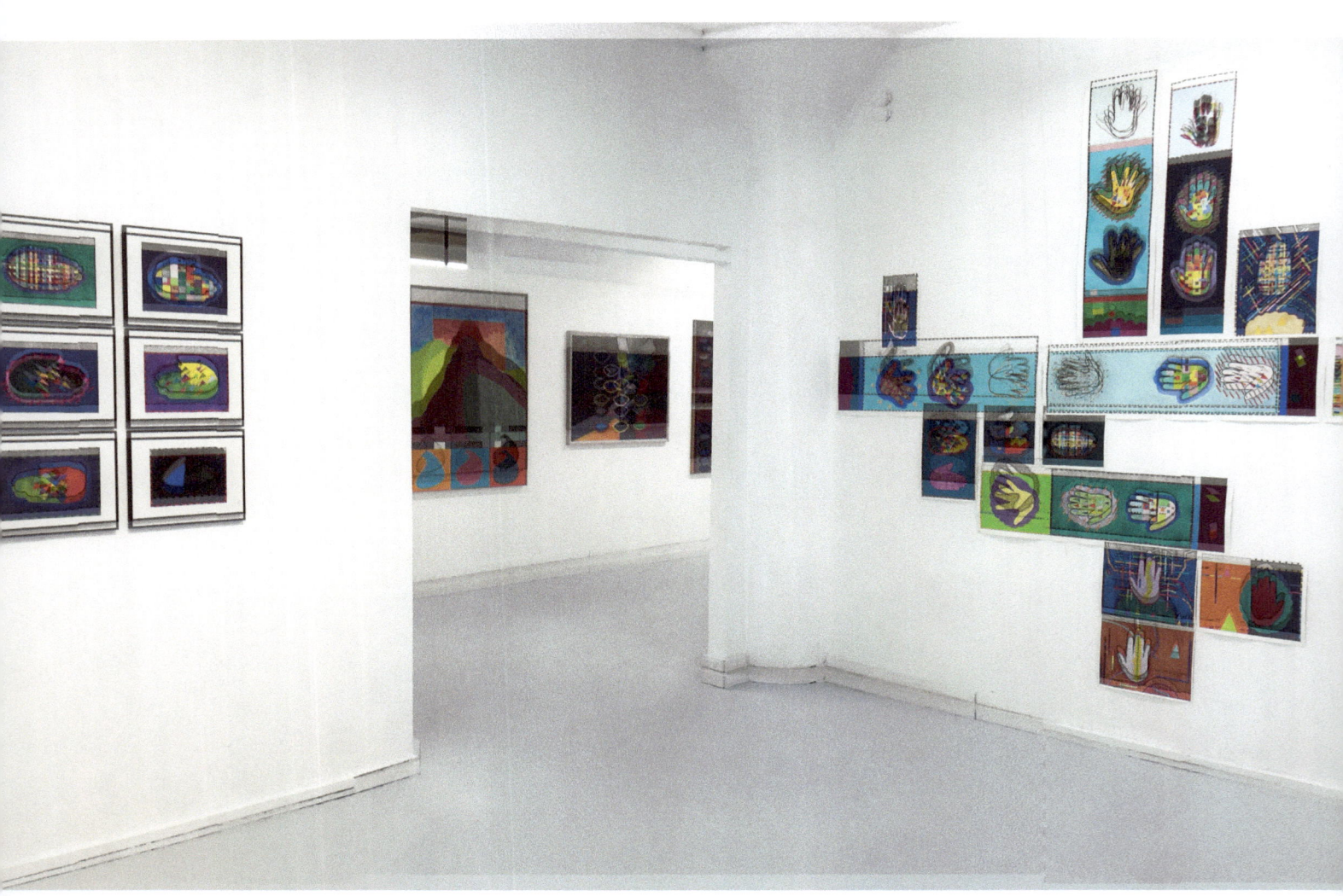

Installation view of *David & Beatrice: Hands and Other Symbols*
Installation view of *David & Beatrice: Hands and Other Symbols*

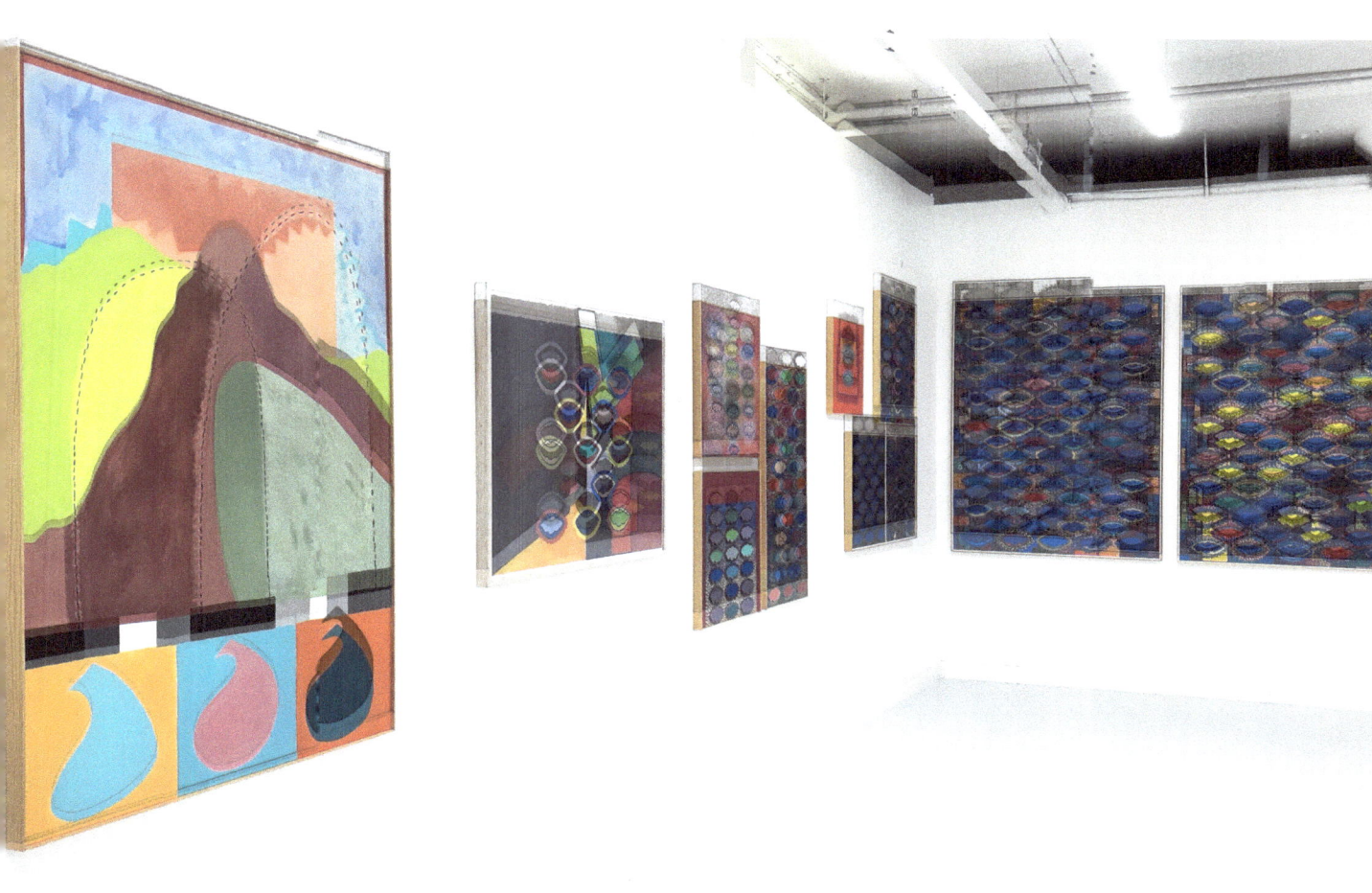

Installation view of *David & Beatrice: Hands and Other Symbols*
Installation view of *David & Beatrice: Hands and Other Symbols*

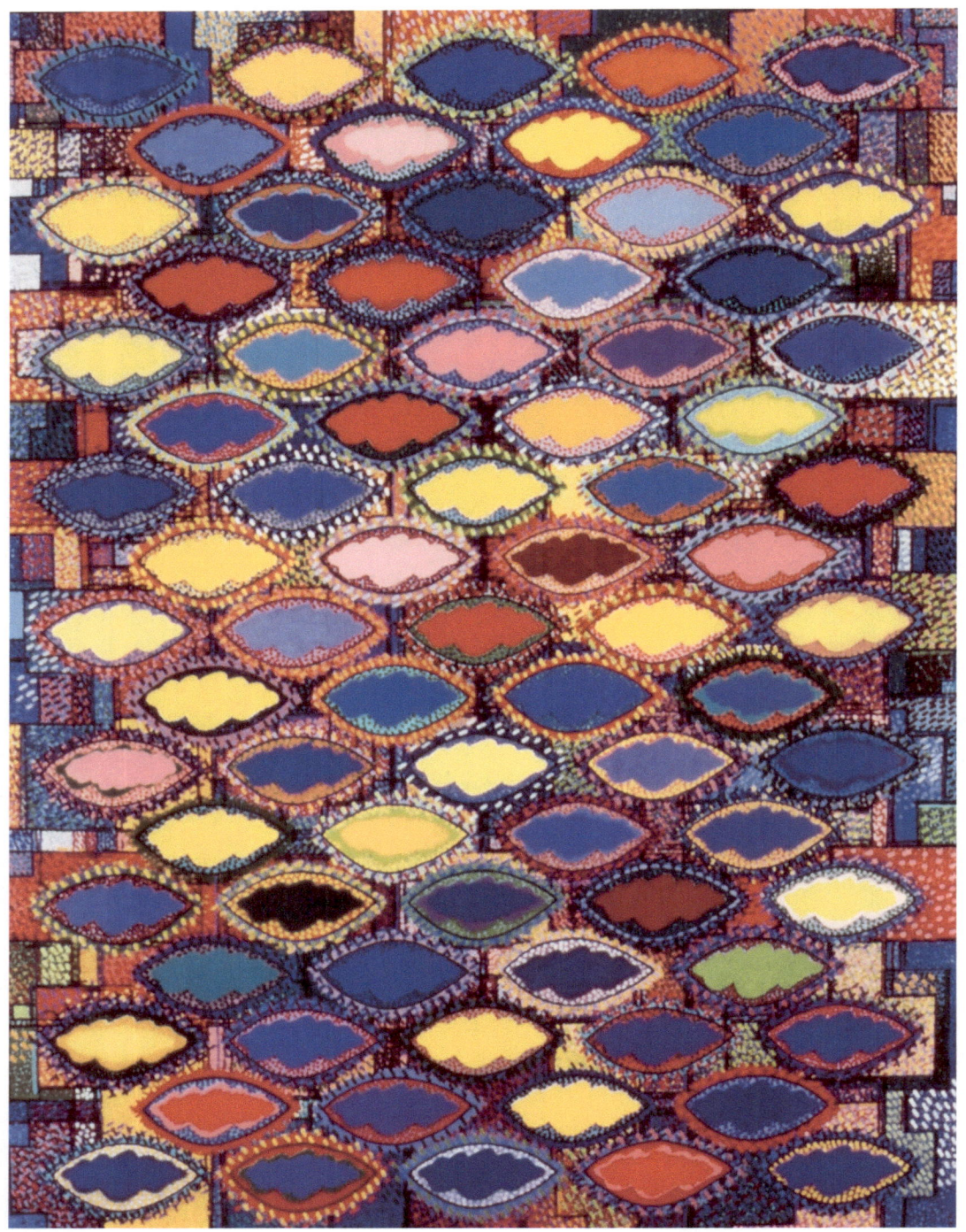
David W. Cummings: Fire in the Hole, oil on panel, 63" x 48", 1988

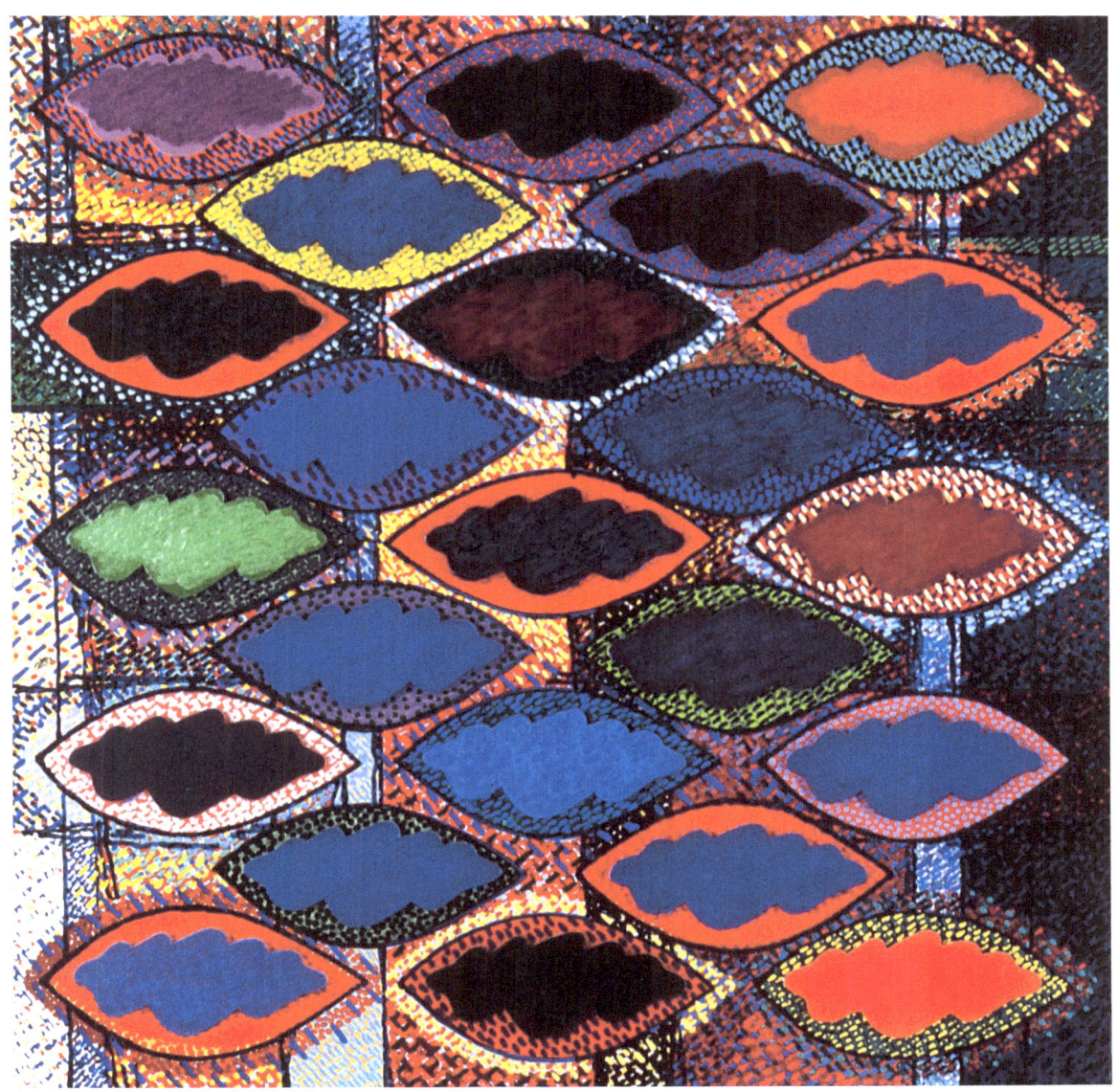

David W. Cummings: Tunder Light, oil on panel, 28" x 28", 1983

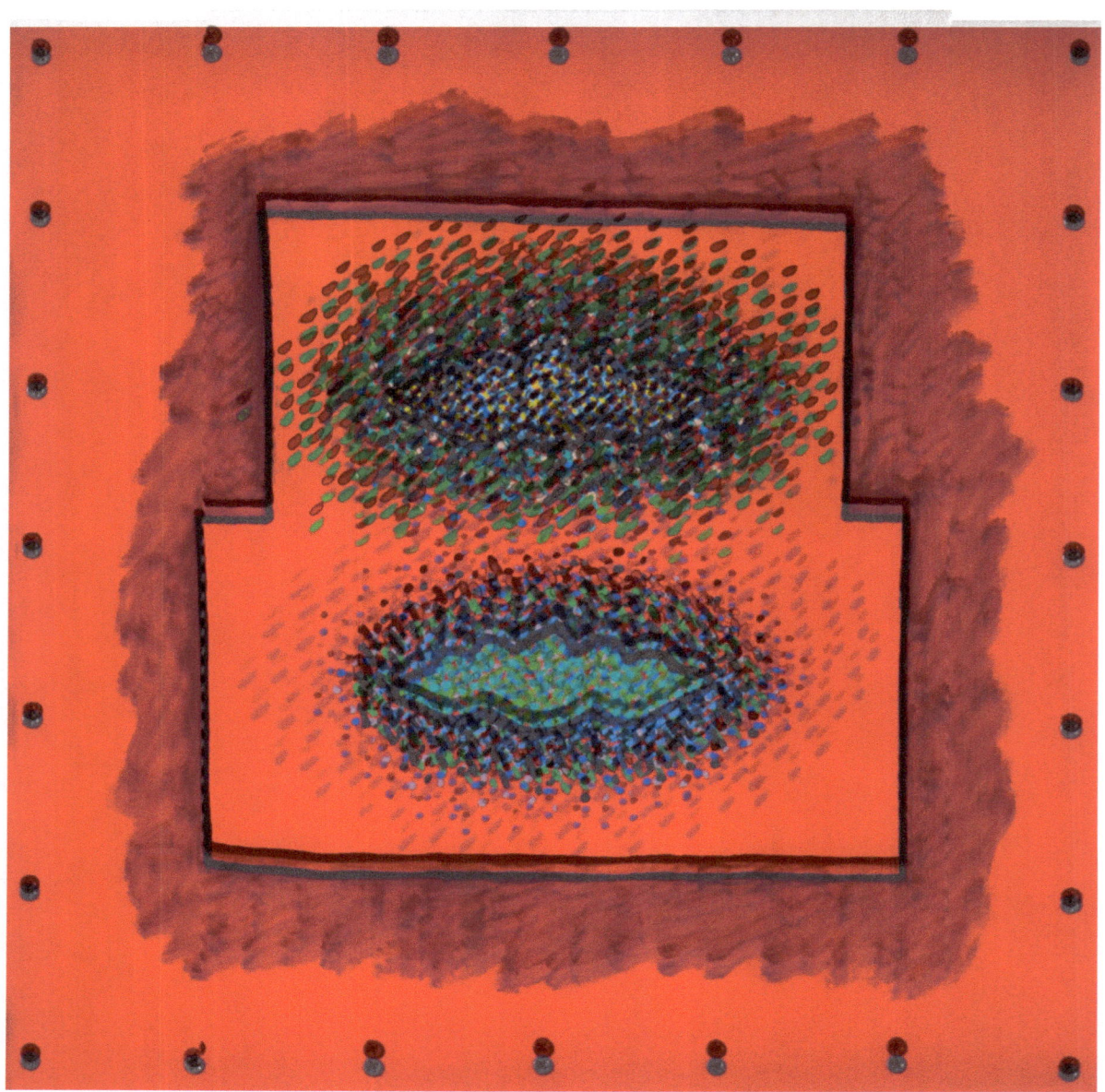

David W. Cummings: Search for a Myth, oil on panel, 18.5" x 18.5", 1982
David W. Cummings: Search for a Myth, oil on panel, 18.5" x 18.5", 1982

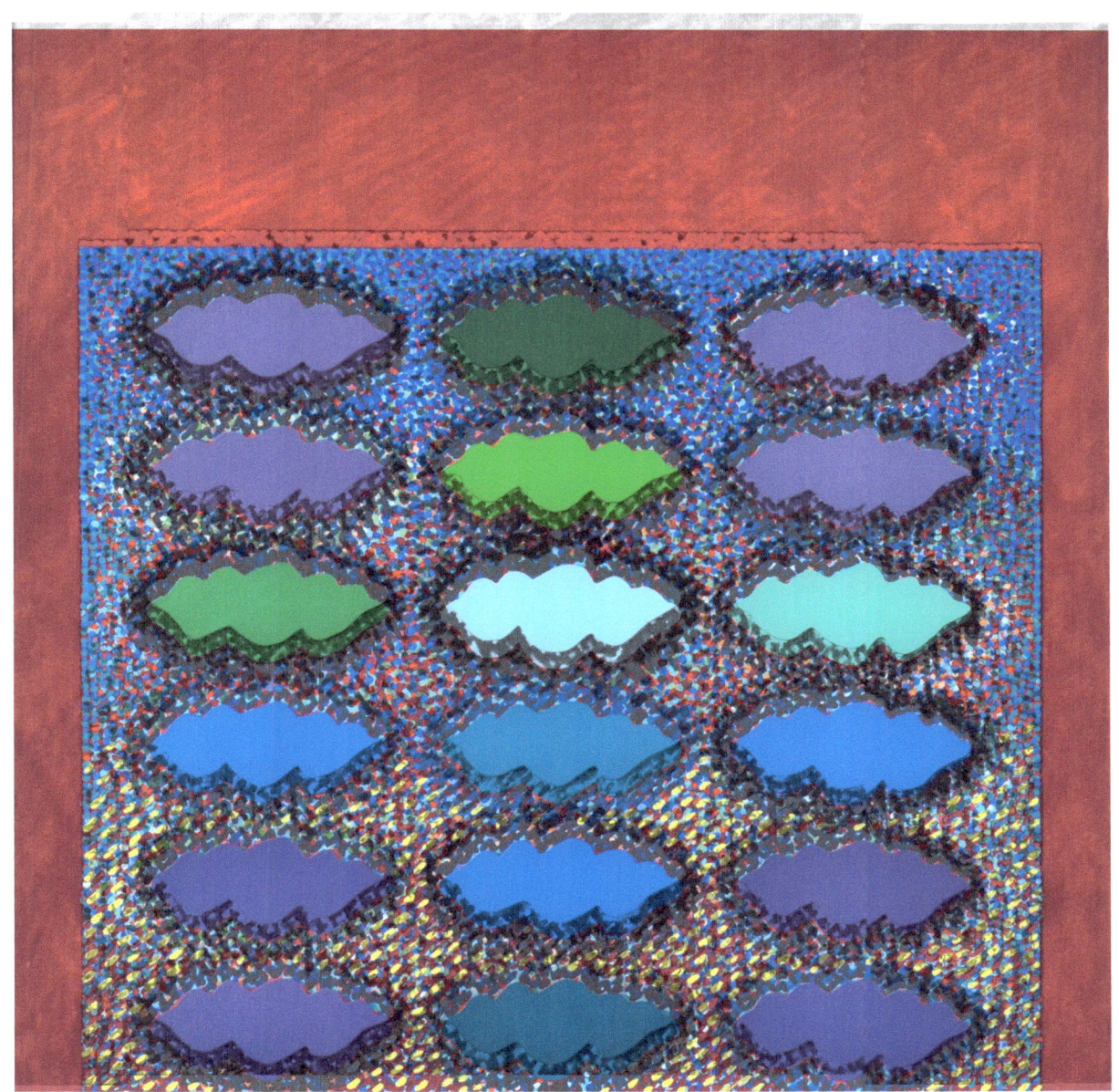

David W. Cummings: Red Semi, oil on panel, 24" x 24", 1980
David W. Cummings: Red Semi, oil on panel, 24" x 24", 1980

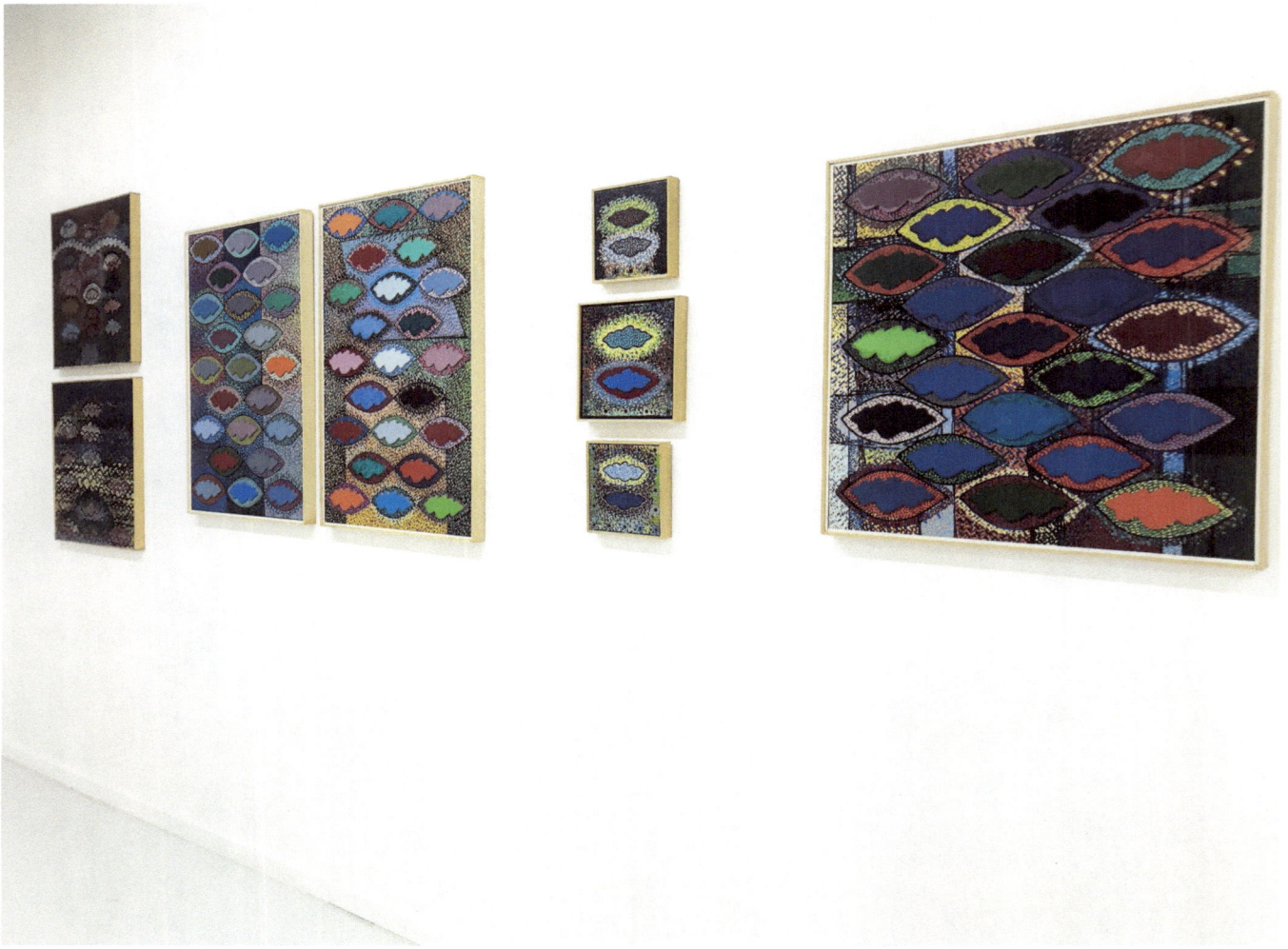

Installation view of *David & Beatrice: Hands and Other Symbols*

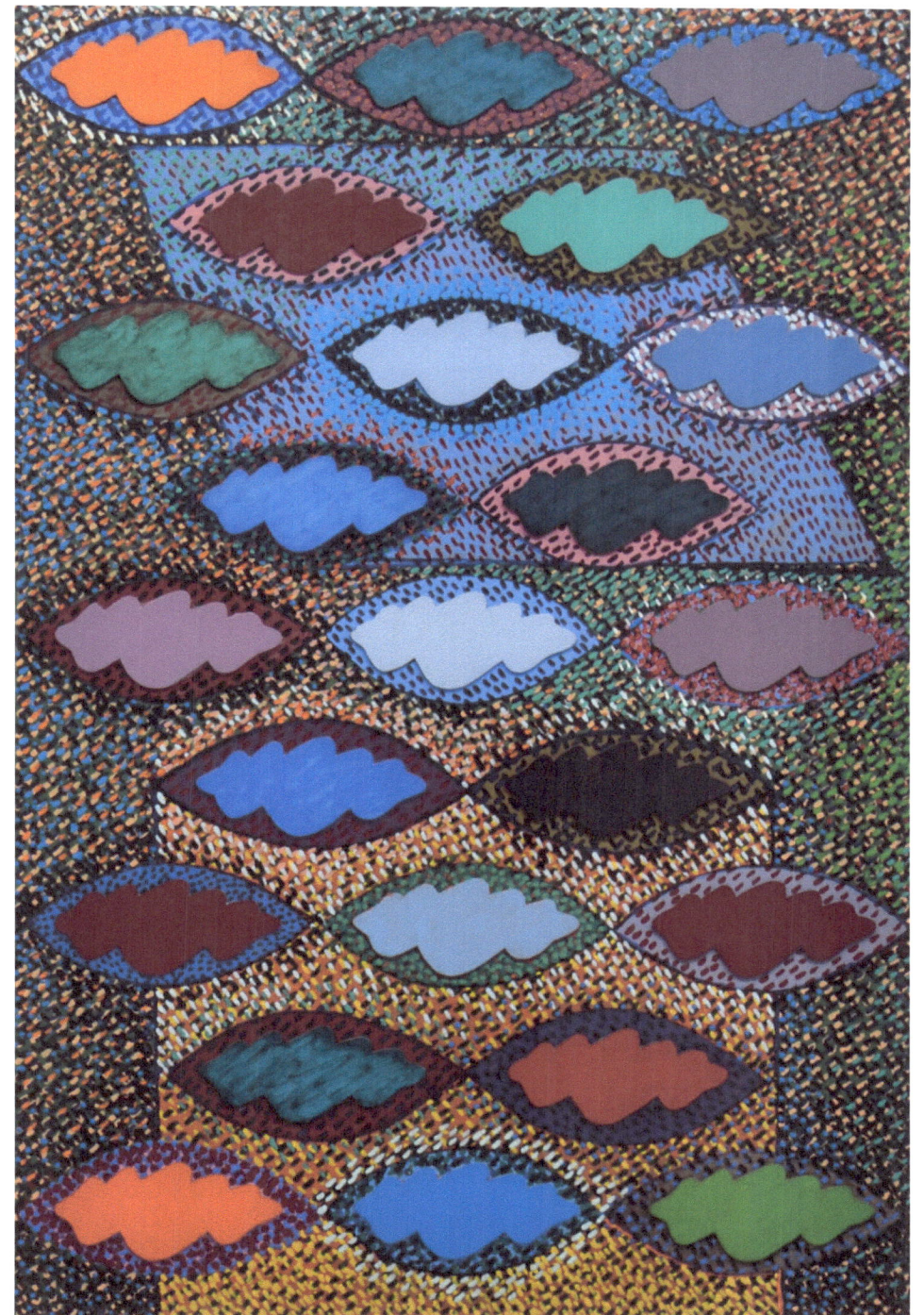

David W. Cummings: Message to Theo, oil on panel, 37" x 26", 1981

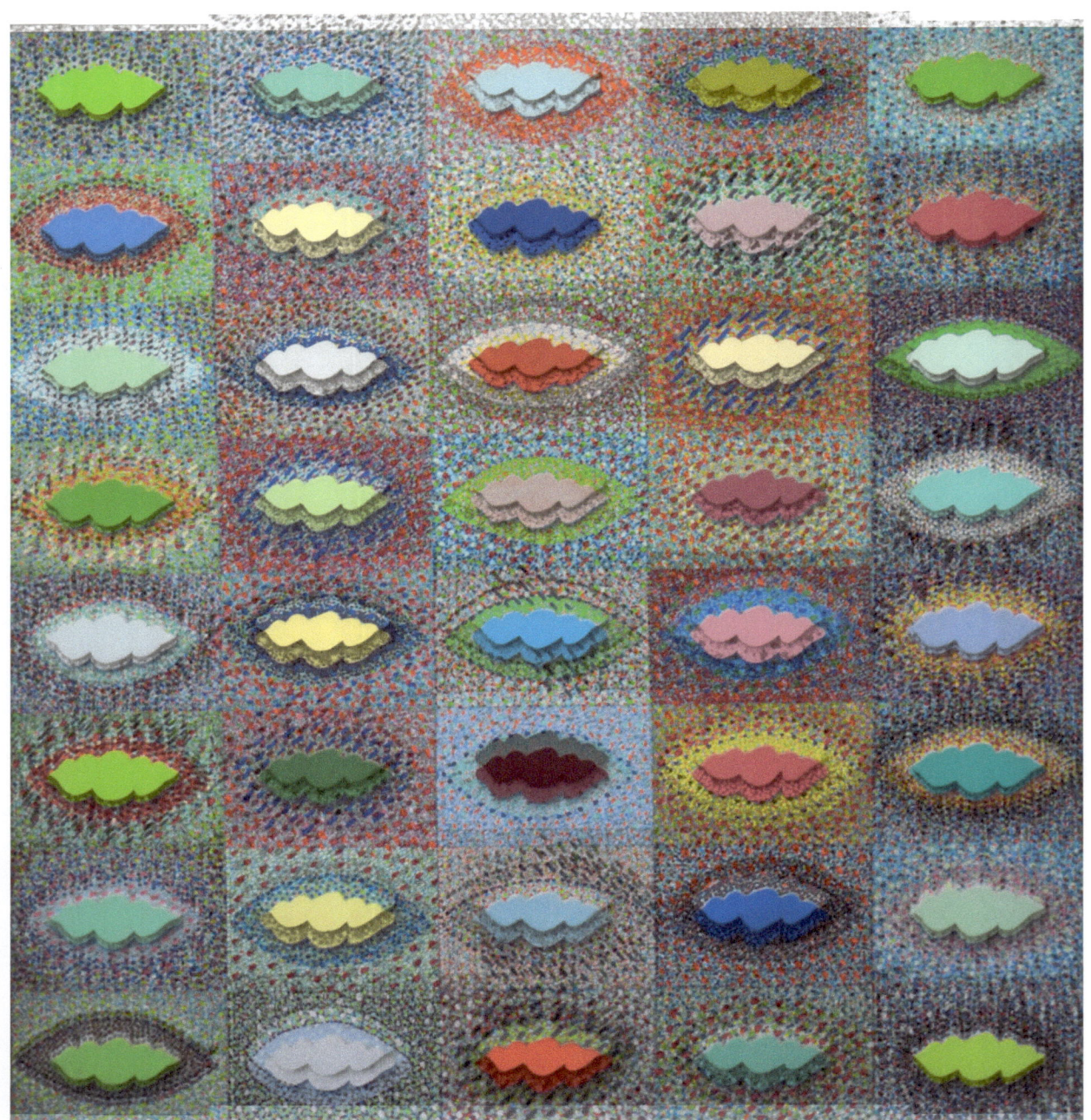

David W. Cummings: Cherokee, oil on panel, 41" x 42", 1979

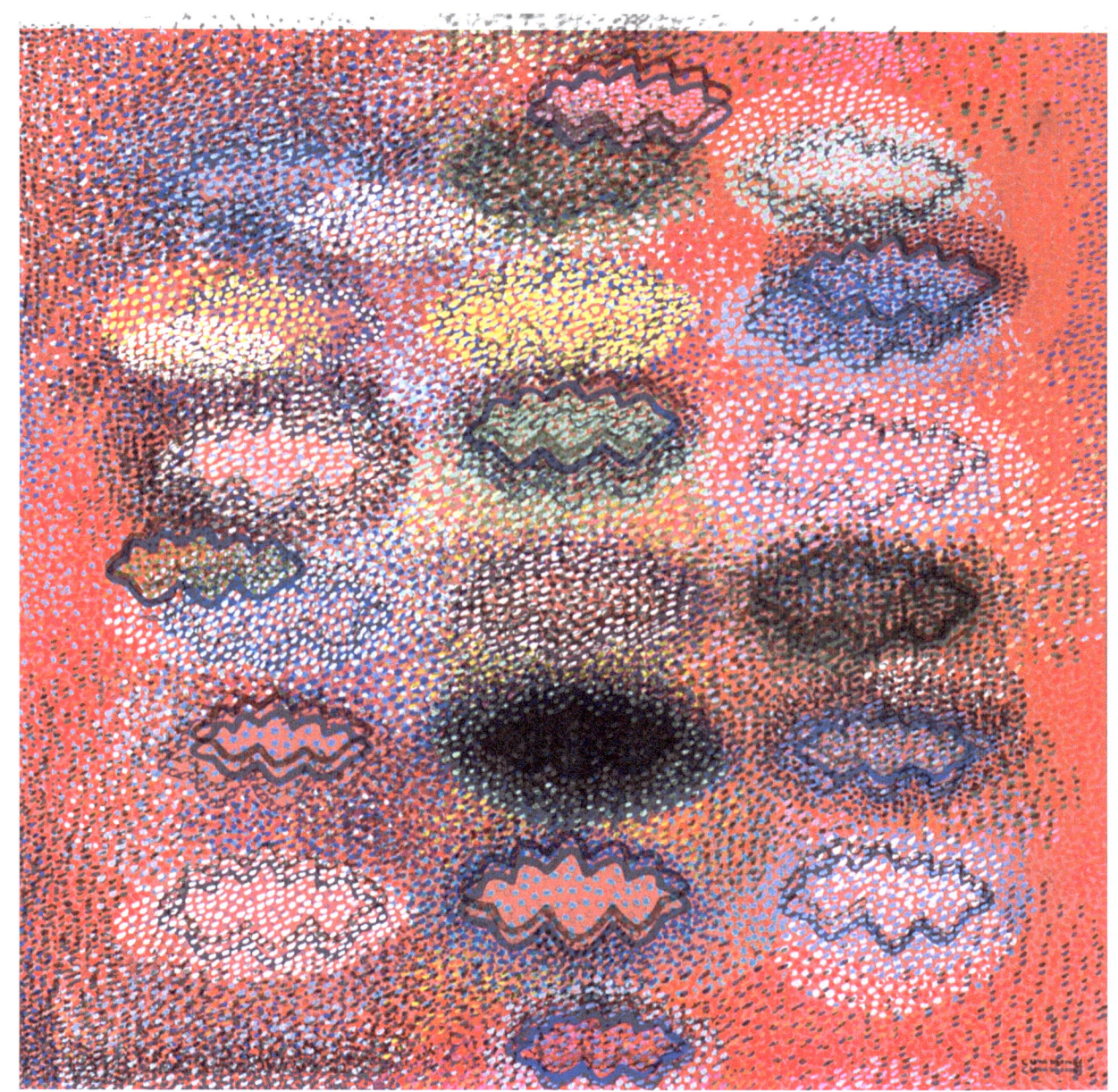

David W. Cummings: Waldorf, oil on panel, 24" x 24", 1975

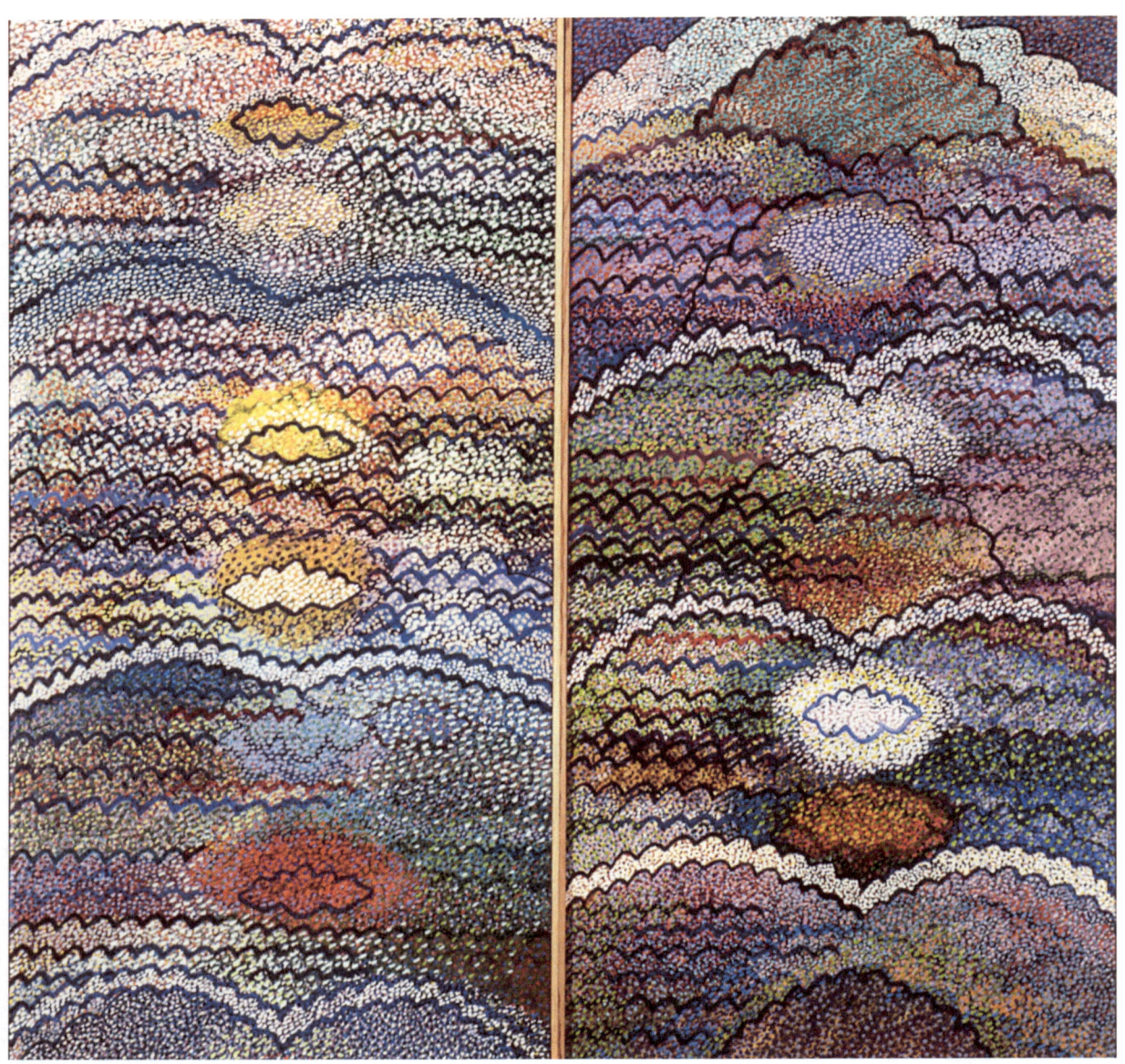

David W. Cummings: Eastern Breeze, oil on panel (diptych), 42" x 40", 1974

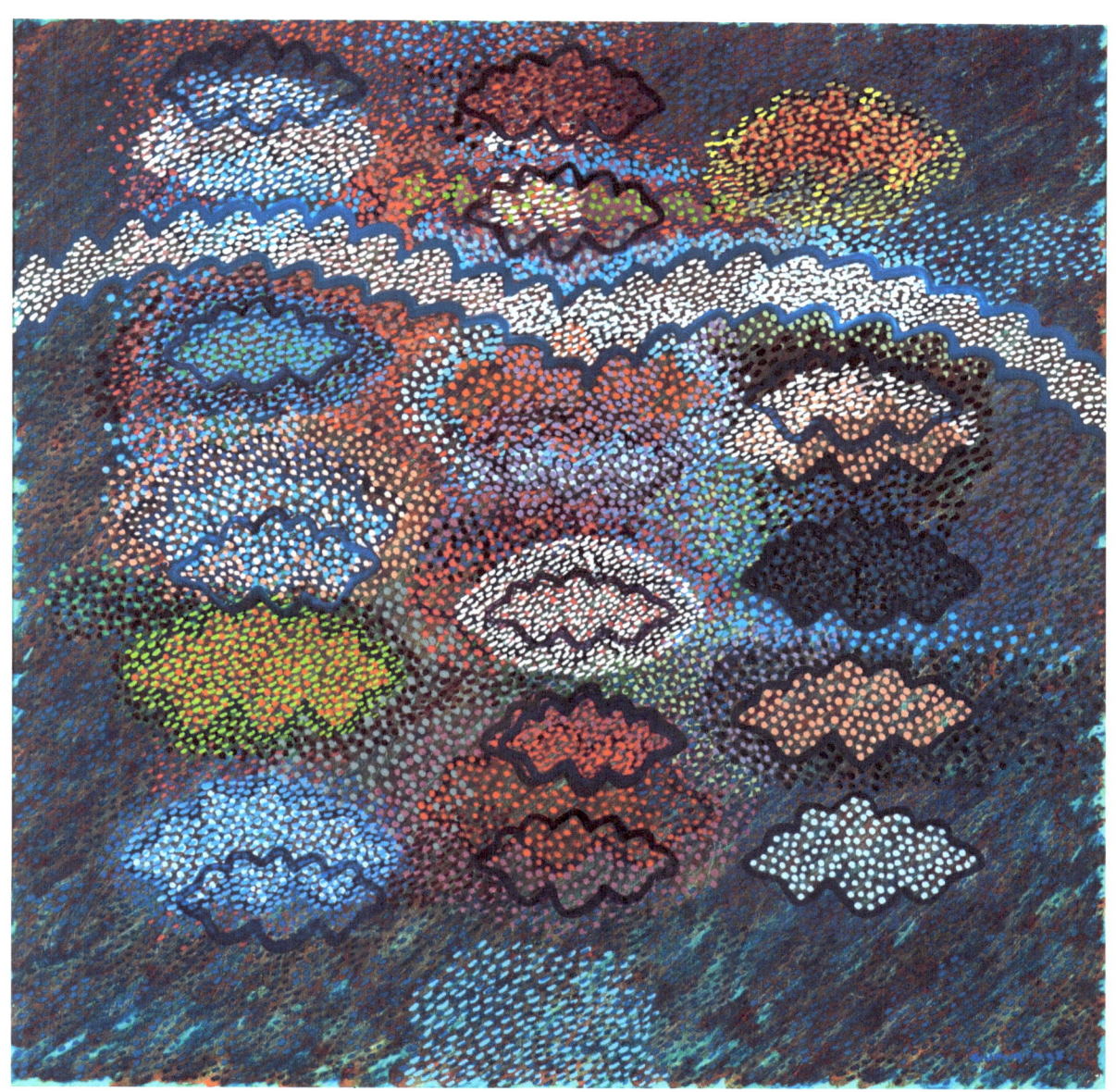

David W. Cummings: Muse of 24th Street, oil on panel, 24" x 24", 1974

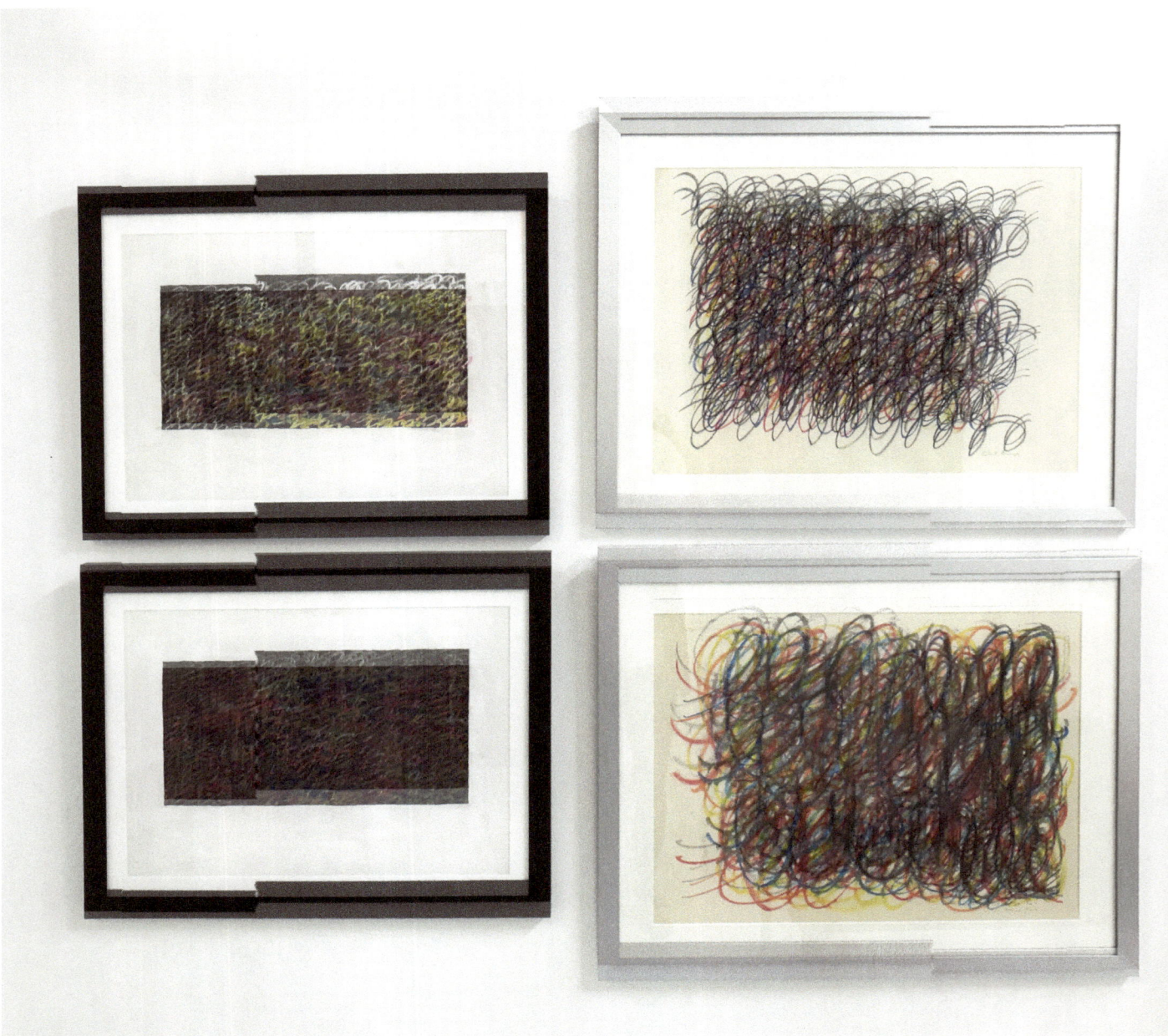

David W. Cummings: Left, Untitled #3, Untitled #2, pastel on paper, 7" x 14", 1970
Right, Untitled 1967 #5, Untitled #2, oil pastel on paper, 18" x 24", 1967

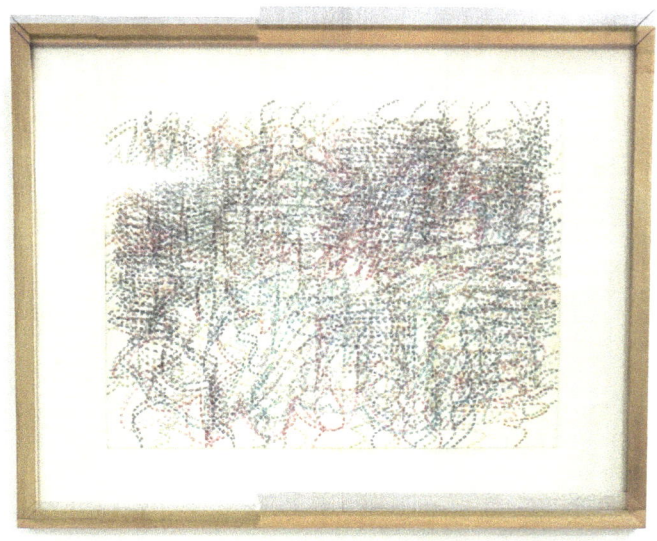

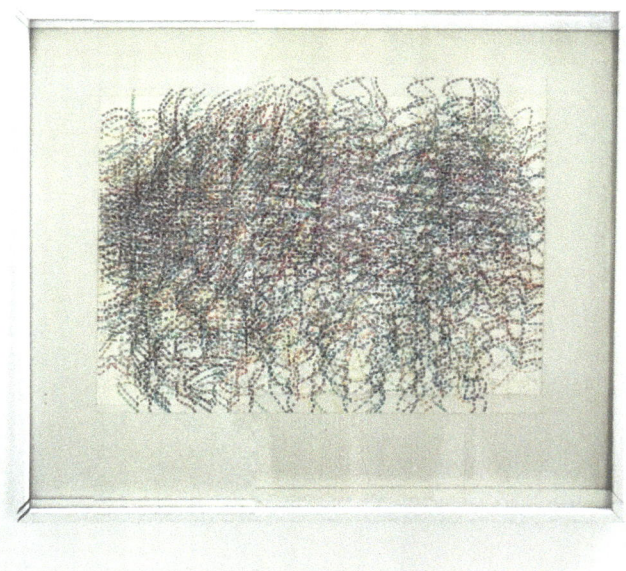

David W. Cummings: Untitled #2, marker on paper, 14" x 16", 1972,
David W. Cummings: Untitled #1, marker on paper, 14" x 16", 1972

David W. Cummings' works are in these public collections:

- Whitney Museum of American Art, New York, New York
- Los Angeles County Museum of Art, Los Angeles, California
- Center for Contemporary Art, Antwerp, Belgium
- Aldrich Museum of Contemporary Art, Ridgefield, Connecticut
- Jeugd en Plastiche Kunst, Ghent, Belgium
- Phoenix Museum of Fine Arts, Phoenix, Arizona
- Memorial Art Gallery, University of Rochester, Rochester, New York
- CIGNA Foundation Museum, Philadelphia, Pennsylvania
- University of North Dakota, Grand Forks, North Dakota
- Sydney and Frances Lewis Foundation, Richmond, Virginia
- Chase Manhattan Collection, New York, New York
- The Port Authority Collection, New York, New York
- Chemical National Collection, New York, New York
- Citibank Collection, New York, New York
- Federal Land Bank Collection, St. Paul, Minnesota
- Rutgers University, Newark, New Jersey
- New Jersey State Museum, Trenton, New Jersey

View more at: https://davidwcummings.net

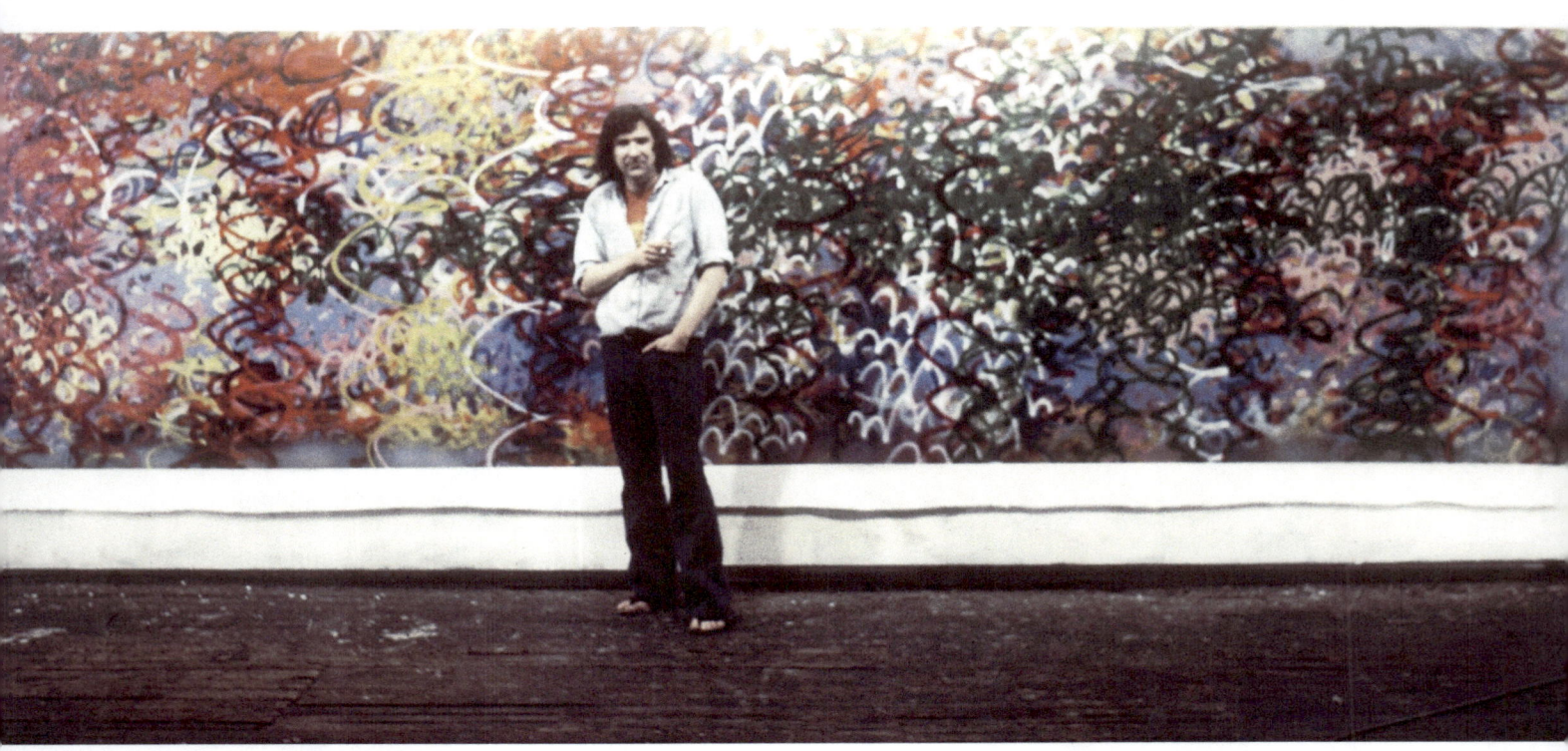

David W. Cummings standing in front of Untitled, acrylic spray painting on canvas, 64" x 129", c.1969
This work is not in the exhibition.

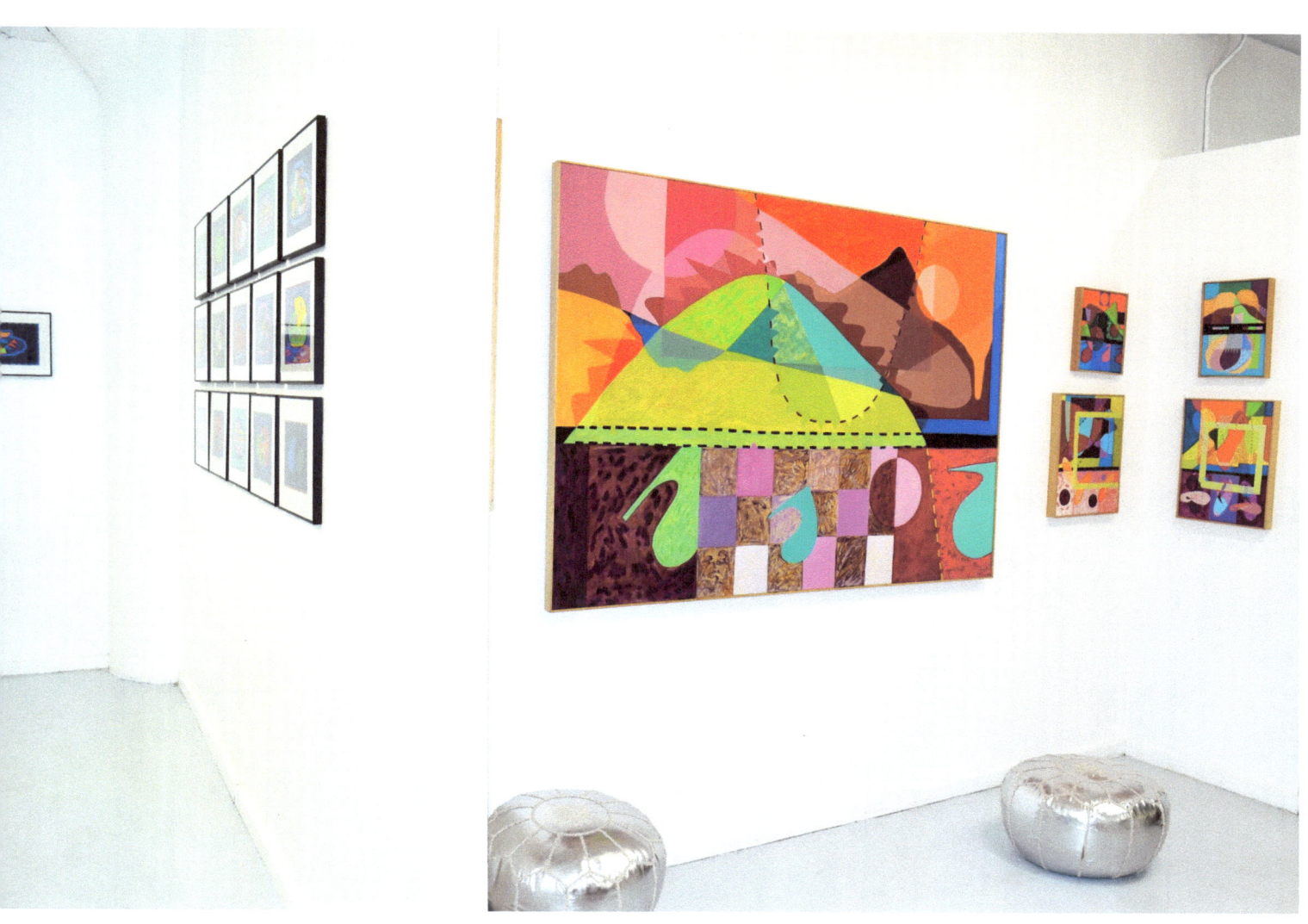

Installation view of *David & Beatrice: Hands and Other Symbols*

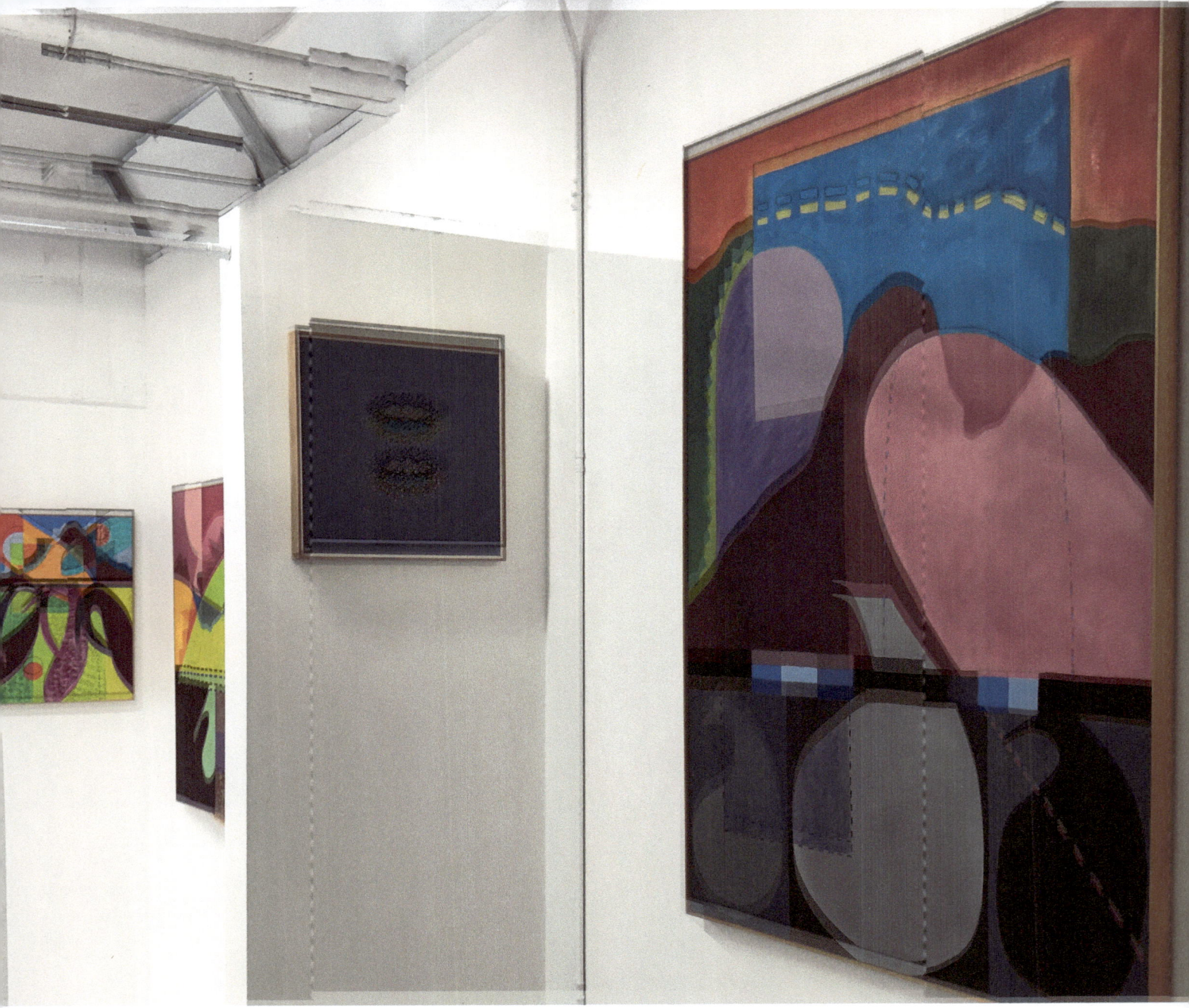

Installation view of *David & Beatrice: Hands and Other Symbols*

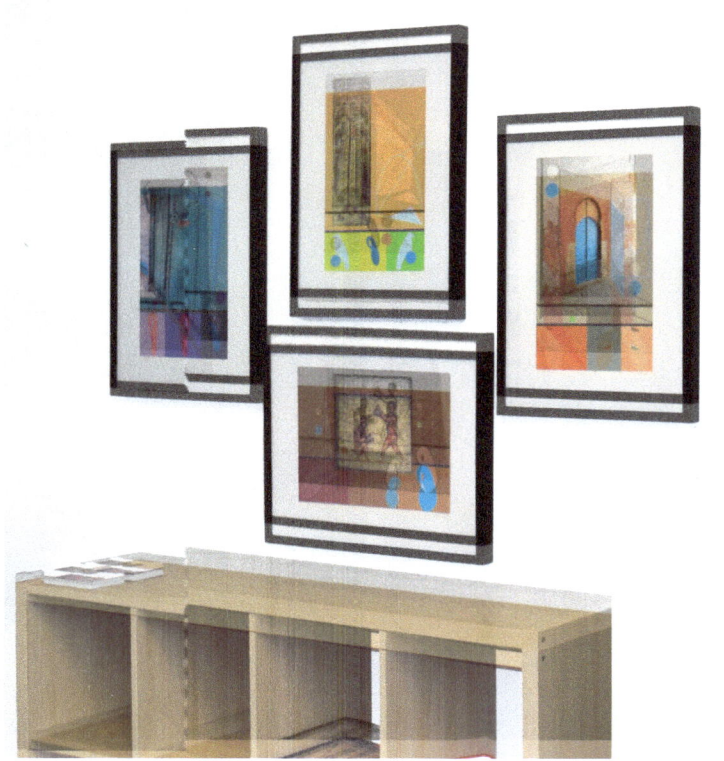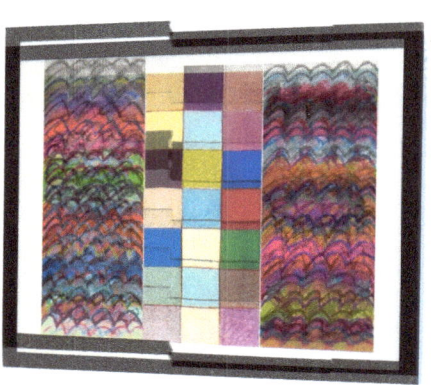

Beatrice M. Mady: 4 digital prints | David W. Cummings: Untitled triptych, pastel on paper, 26" x 32", 1973

Ideas are sparked from things I see on my travels or events in my life. I might be made aware of new patterns, colors and light or I try to express visually ideas for which I have no words. In the studio, these notions present themselves in ways that I do not always expect.

Color is my main voice. My paintings have always been about texture and pattern, a task I accomplish by using gestural brushstrokes and impastos. The color is in constant dialogue with the drawn images in layers that are both with opaque and transparent. In the paintings I adhere to the purity of abstraction.

Beatrice M. Mady, 2020

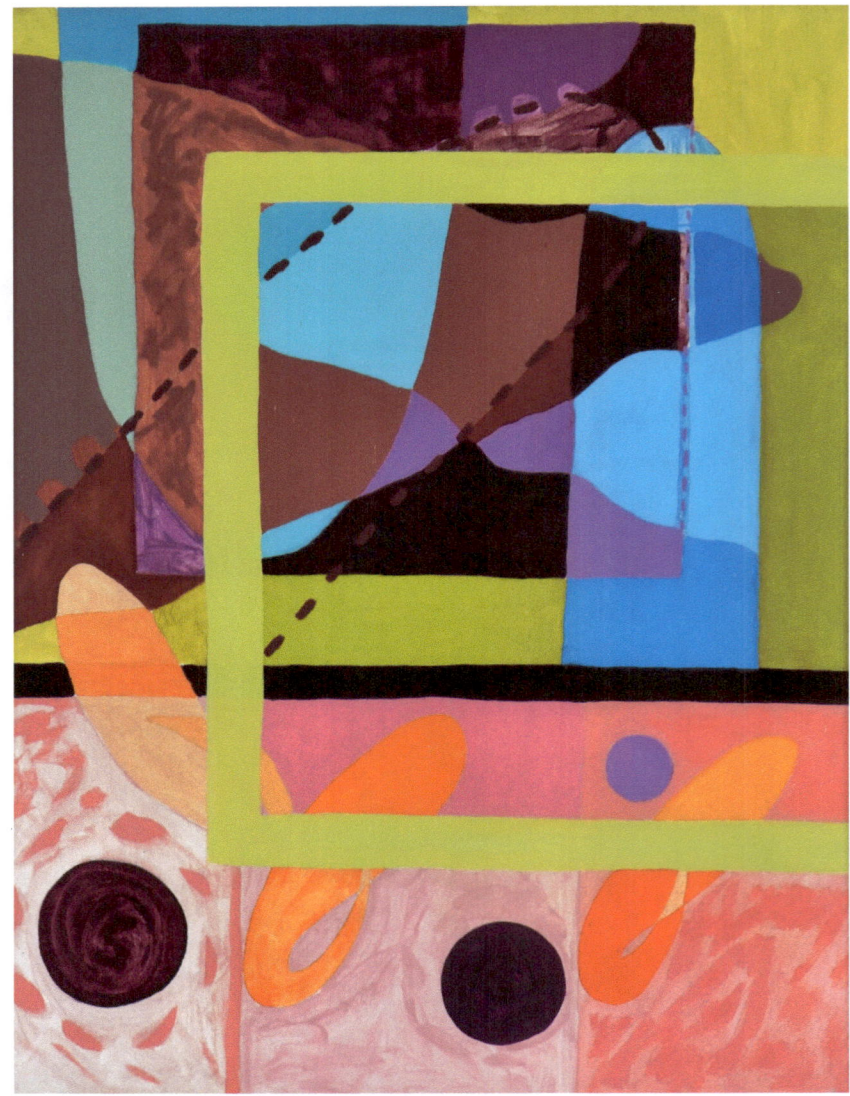

Beatrice M. Mady: Pentatonic Scales, oil on canvas, 18" x 14", 2009

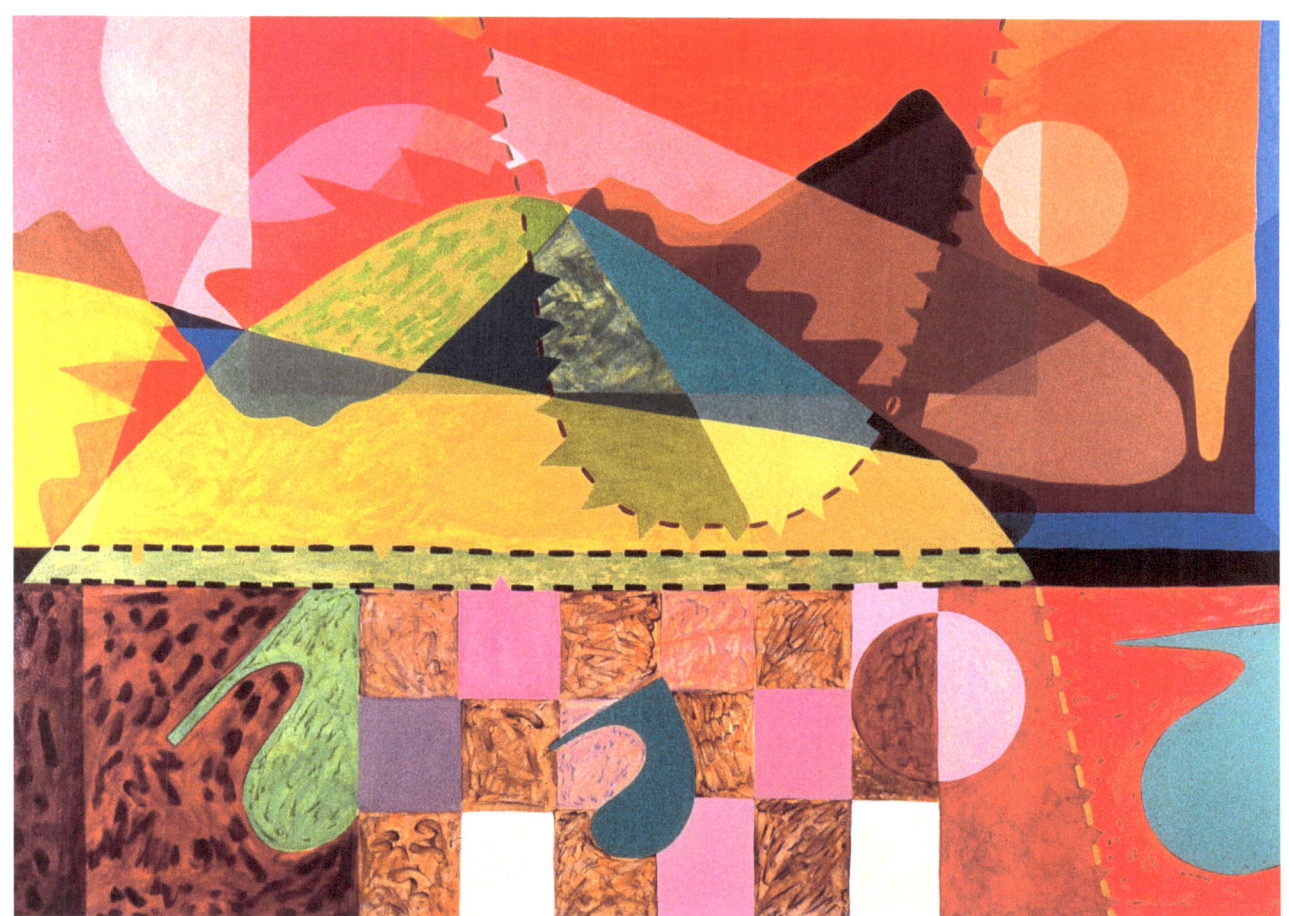

Beatrice M. Mady: Giotto's Angels, oil on canvas, 48" x 66", 1996

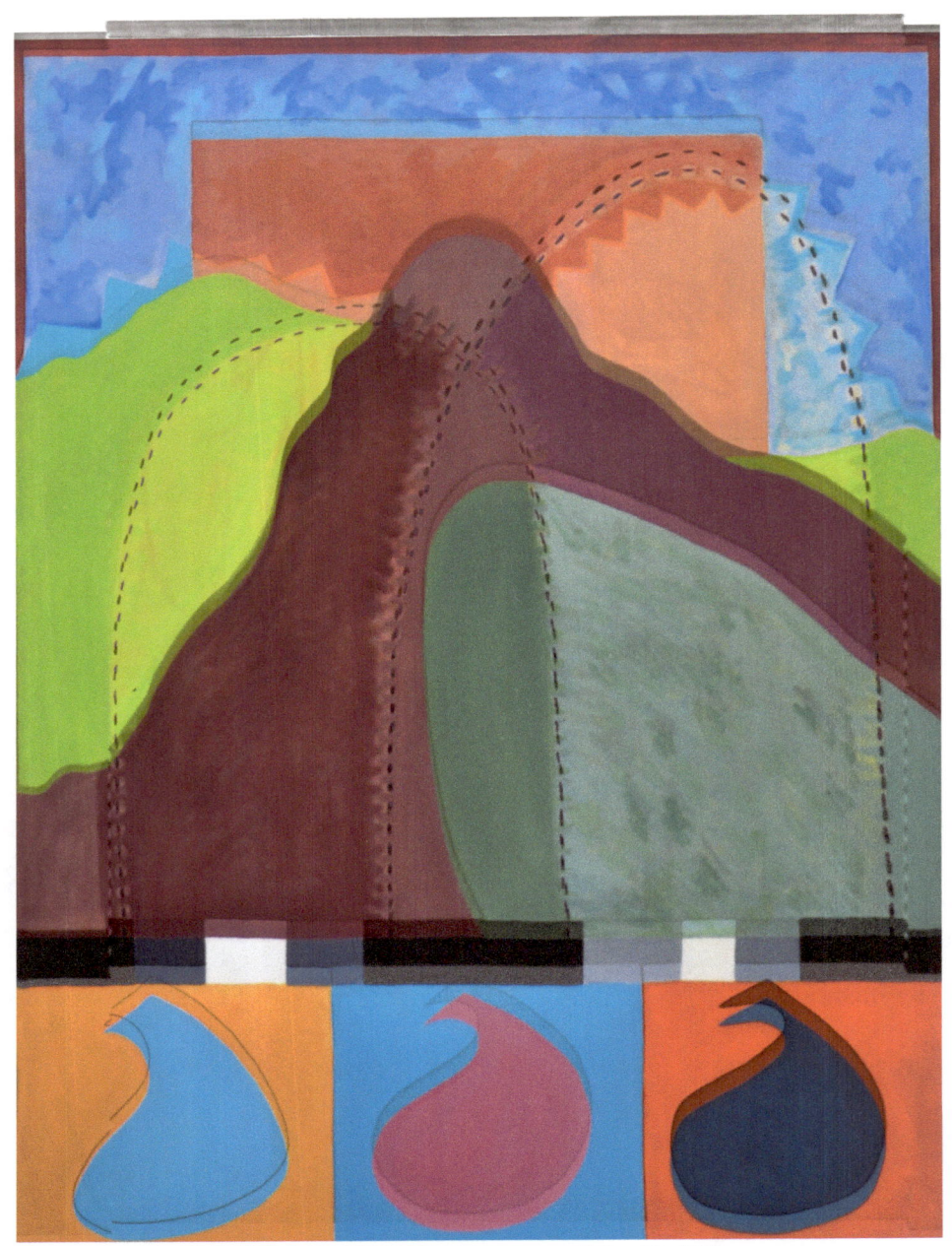

Beatrice M. Mady: Yggdrasil, oil on canvas, 54" x 40", 1992
Beatrice M. Mady: Yggdrasil, oil on canvas, 54" x 40", 1992

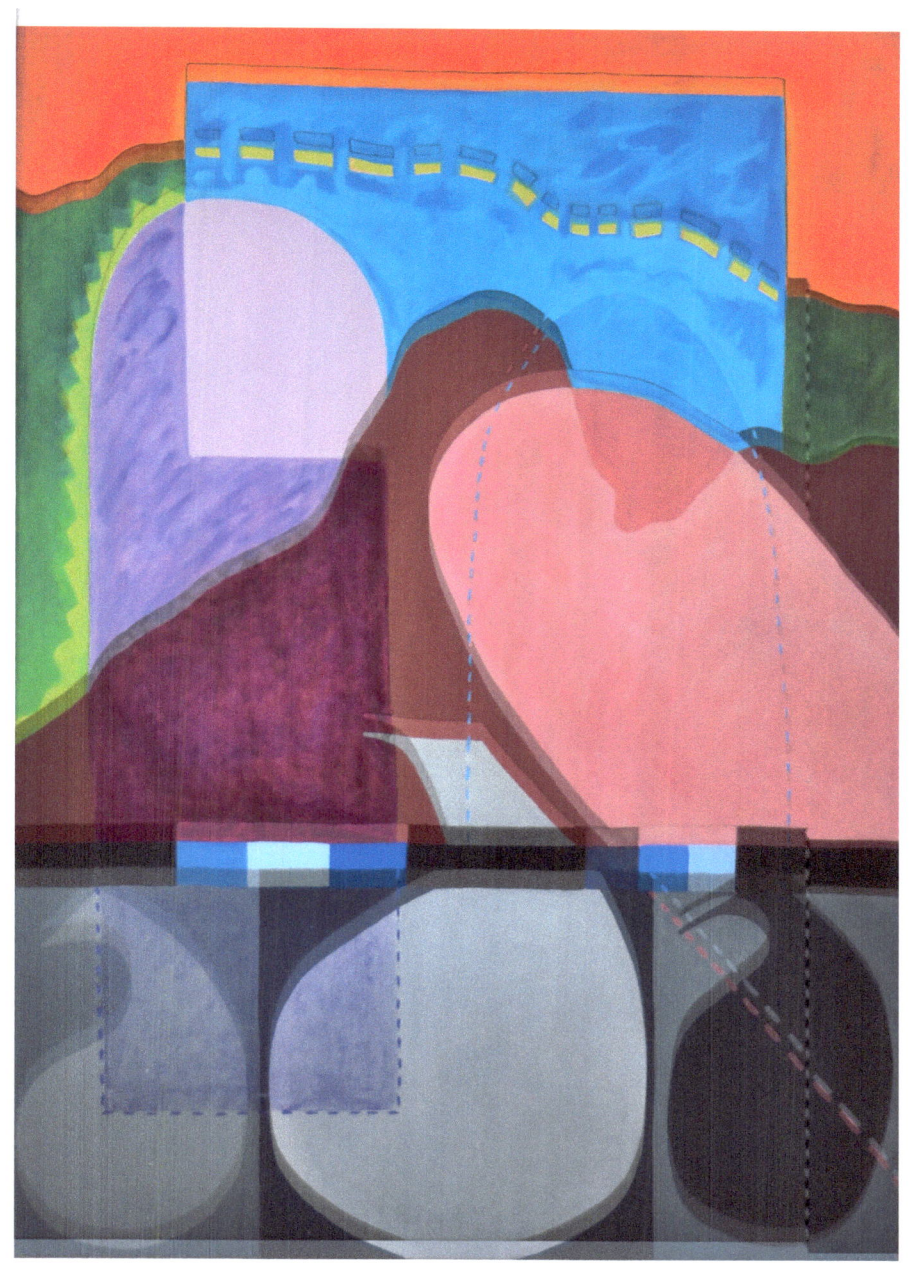

Beatrice M. Mady: Ruler of the Spirits, oil on canvas, 60" x 42", 1992

Beatrice M. Mady is a digital artist and painter currently living and working in Jersey City, New Jersey. She received a M.F.A. in painting from Pratt Institute and a B.F.A. from the University of Dayton.

Her works are on view in museums such as the Dayton Art Institute, Museum of Friends and Drew University Museum, and in corporate collections: Pfizer, Ortho Dermatological, Janssen Pharmaceutics, Bristol-Meyers Squibb, Johnson and Johnson, Sydney and Francis Lewis Foundation, Arenol Chemical Corporation, Capital Health Medical Center, The Provident Bank of NJ, PNC Bank and in private collections.

She was a recipient of a Ford Foundation Grant, a New Jersey State Council on the Arts Grant and several Kenny Grants.

Ms. Mady is a Professor, the Graphic Arts Coordinator and Gallery Director of the Fine Arts Gallery at Saint Peter's University in Jersey City, New Jersey.

View more work at:
http://www.beatricemady.com

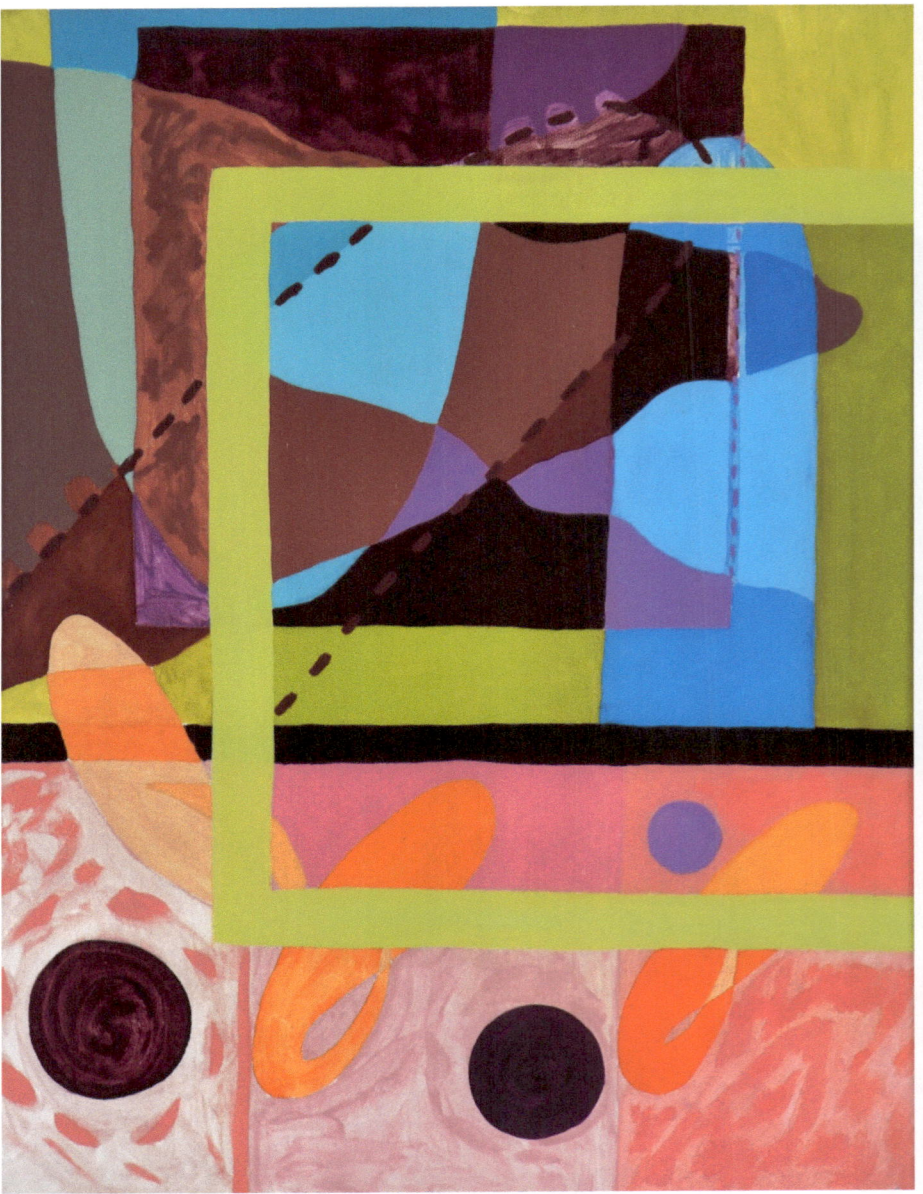

Beatrice M. Mady: Burning in the Shadows, oil on canvas, 18" x 14", 2009

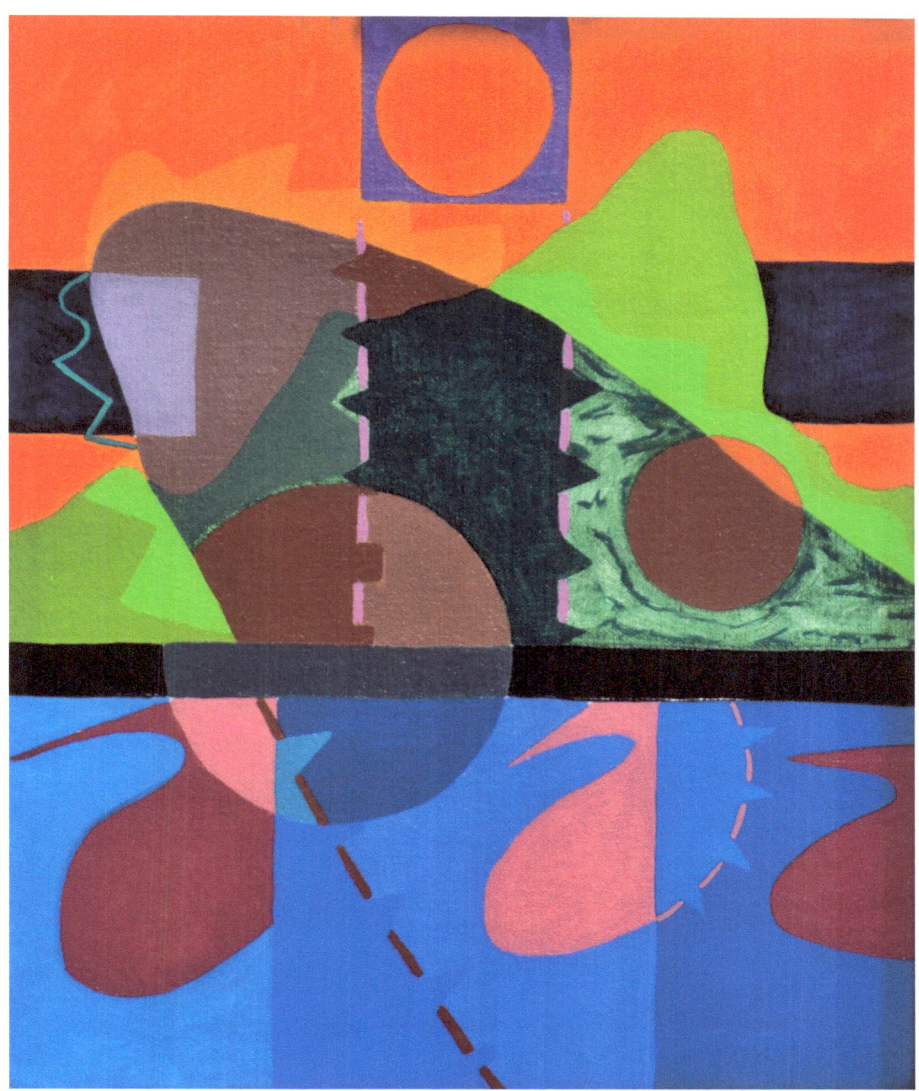

Beatrice M. Mady: Hecate, oil on canvas, 12" x 10", 1996

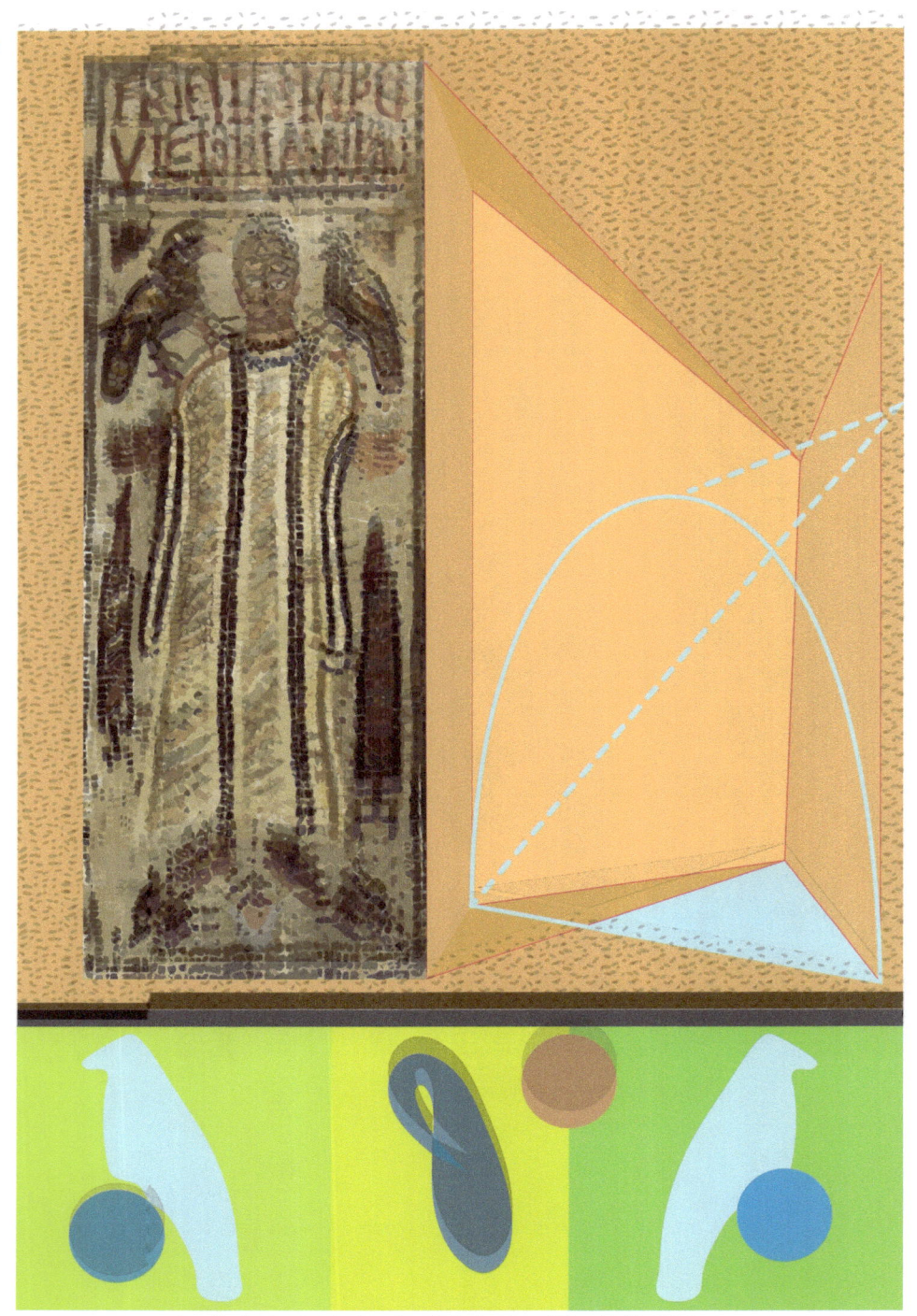

Béatrice M. Mady: Bardo Mosaic, digital print, 17" x 11.5", 2020

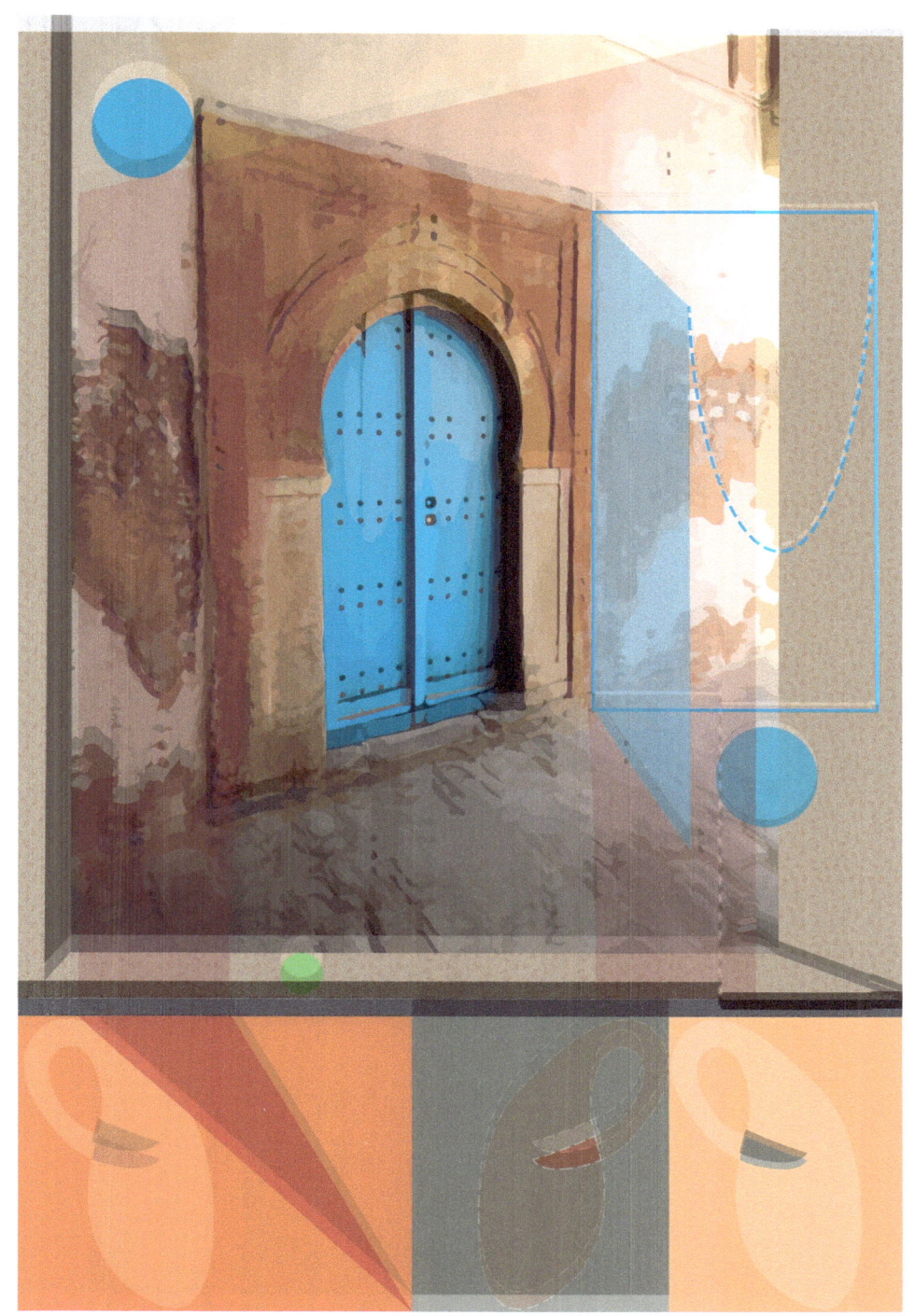

Beatrice M. Mady: Another Blue Door, digital print, 17" x 11.5", 2020

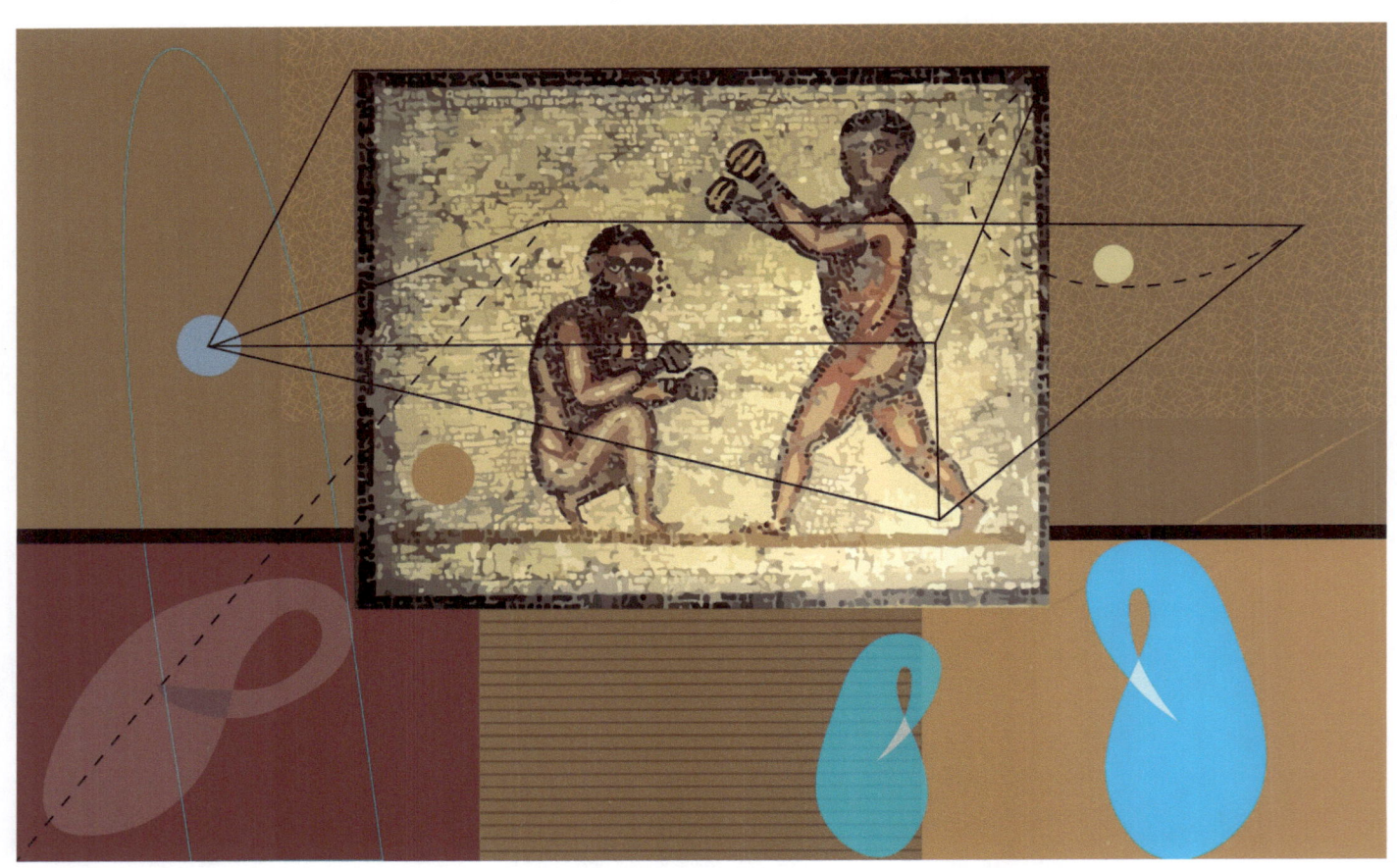

Beatrice M. Mady: Knock Out, digital print, 11.5" x 17", 2020

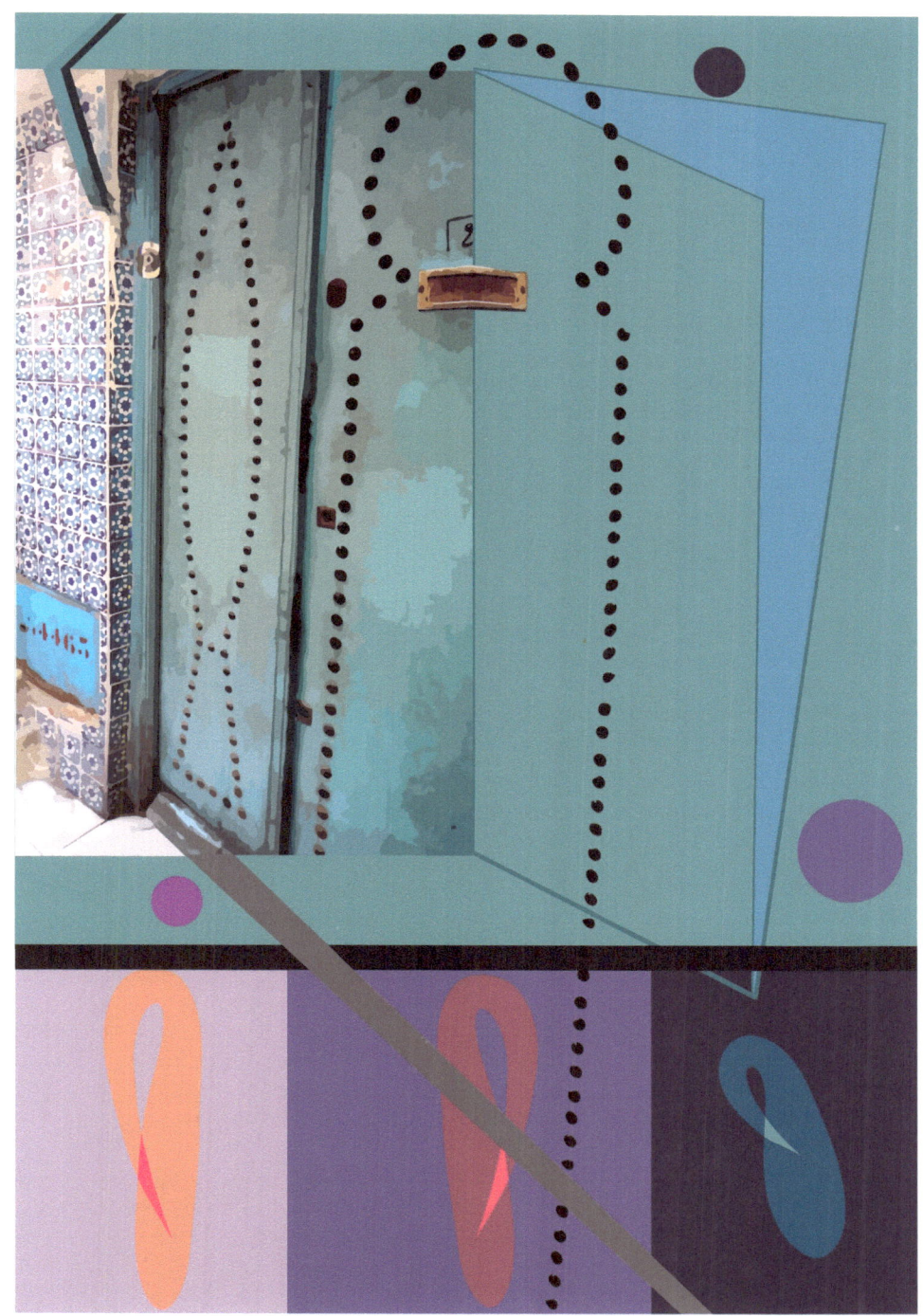

Beatrice M. Mady: Further East By the Sea, digital print, 17" x 11.5", 2020

This is a show about duality, primarily a tension between Modernist tradition and Romantic freedom. The joy of the work asserts that you can have your cake and, after all, eat it too.

David's roots were in an orthodox allegiance to a classical style loyal to the majesty of the grid and the primacy of flatness and the picture plane. But he also harbored an unruly urge to rococo exuberance. His muse was Cezanne, who loved stable structure above all, but lit an iconoclastic fire that radically engulfed the world of art.

David's work follows a stately trajectory from pure color field abstraction toward a hybrid of formalism and image-making. *In Fire in the Hole* (1988), a phalanx of shapes threaten a color riot that in lesser hands would jostle for attention, but here suggest a well-orchestrated symphony. In an earlier work, *Eastern Breeze* (1974), we glimpse the genesis of these signature "cloud" shapes. This seminal work has a pointillist buzz and manic energy that is harnessed and brought to heel in subsequent paintings. In *Montauk* and *In Harm's Way* (1993), the once sacrosanct picture plan is fragmented, no doubt in homage to the beloved Cezanne and Cubism's coming storm.

With the advent of the hand paintings in the 1990s, David moved decisively from a flirtation with figuration to an embrace. Abstraction still ruled the roost, mind you, but the hand shapes can no longer claim anonymity. They are "portraits" of specific people, though often that person is the artist himself. The hand image refers to a symbol of human self-expression ubiquitous from paleolithic times to the children's art rooms of today, and to the hand-eye relationship essential to the artist.

The large wall installation made up of hand paintings on paper showcases David's mastery of rhythm, harmony, and radiant color. A number of paintings pair male and female hands— duality again. The central image of *Witch Hunter* (2015) with its wild tapestry of color and explosive mandala exemplifies David at his delightful and daring best. David is a master of many media. Whether pastels, markers, watercolor, or oil, every work dances joyfully.

In Beatrice's paintings and digital prints, she explores modernist ideas with emphases on evocative shapes and interlocking lines and, just as with David, luminous color is supreme. There is a clear division between the upper and lower sectors in each oil painting. This demarcation is straight and level and mostly painted black. In most cases, the palette of the lower region is more somber, as befitting a quasi-underworld. The space is often populated by a trio or trios of shapes recruited from the artist's personal iconography.

Though some of her recurring images have their origins in representational sources, Beatrice thinks of them as purely abstract shapes. In *The Dead Can Dance*, Beatrice veers closest to a narrative interpretation, and this tension between symbol and abstraction is arresting. With pelican-like shapes roosting in the under story and skeletal fragments lurking above, there is more than a hint of the dark and tragic haunting this powerful painting.

The circle is another favorite shape hearkening back to Plato's symbol of the cosmos. The back-story is that Beatrice's engineer father gave her his compass set; her early fascination with this magical tool has influenced her work ever since.

In recent digital work, her love of antiquity and Matisse are pervasive. Arabesques of Tunisian architecture are overlaid with complementary lines and abstract shapes. Photo images of ethereal art from the real world are matched and conjoined with pure abstraction.

"Painting is another form of thinking,'" according to Gerhard Richter. Perhaps there is an implication here of a fundamental duality in the life of an artist. The artist thinks and functions like everyone else in their everyday world, but in the studio a transformation, possibly miraculous—can occur.

Phillip Guston described this idea in an interview with Robert Storr: In the studio the artist is alone with Velasquez, Picasso, and all the great masters he admires. Then one by one they leave—and if he is truly engaged, "even he leaves."

To inhabit that zone, even if only fleetingly, is the greatest fringe benefit of a creative life. This exhibition is replete with evidence that both Beatrice and David often experienced that altered and exalted state.

Essay by Peter Delman
Nieuw Art Blog, March, 13, 2020

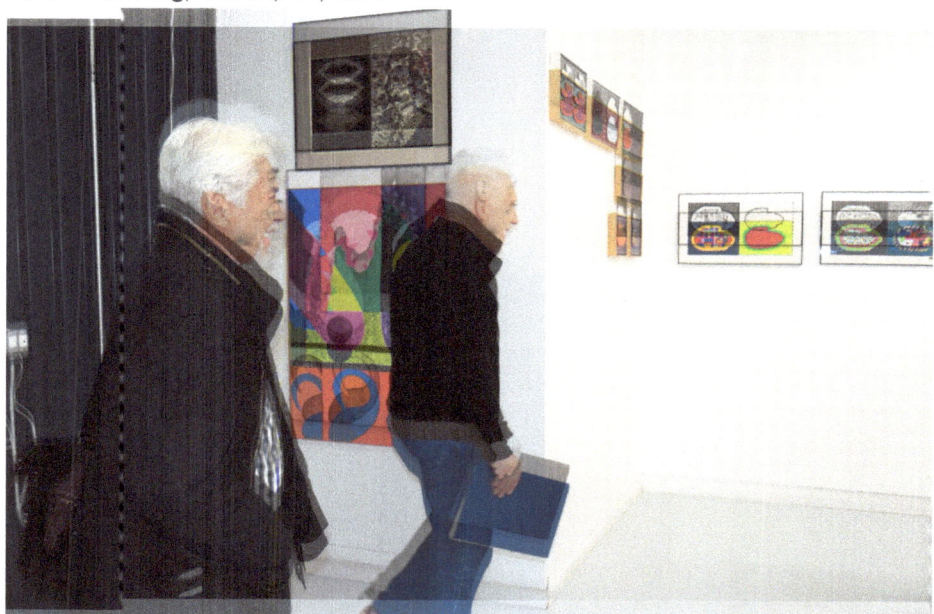

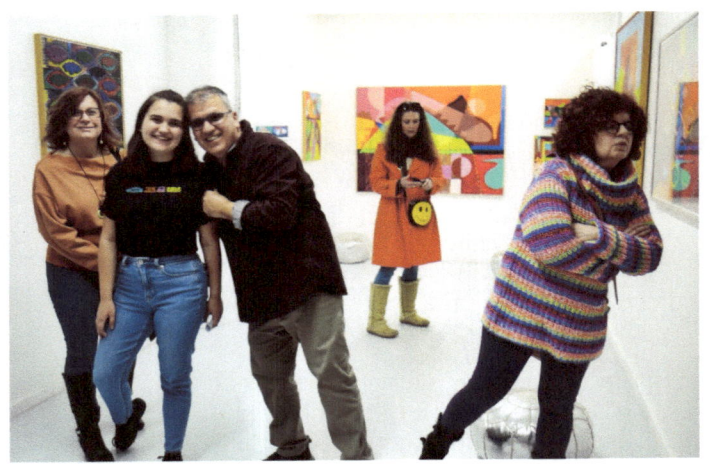
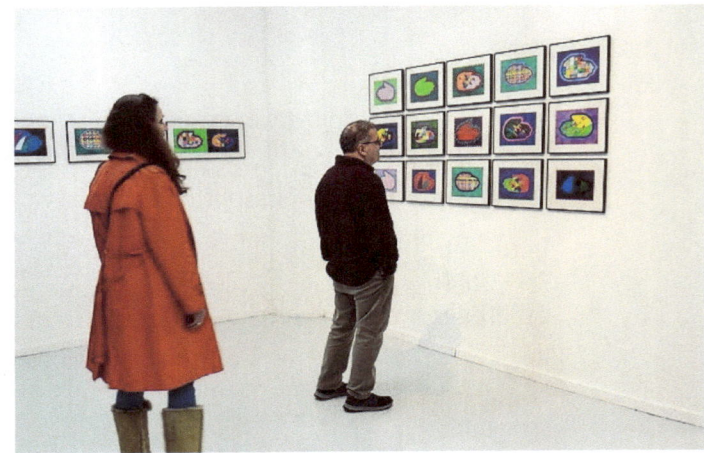
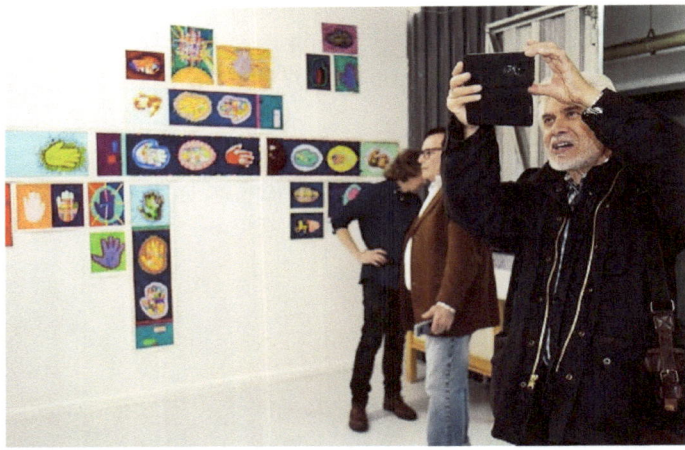

VICTORY HALL PRESS
Drawing Rooms 926 Newark Avenue #T107
Jersey City, New Jersey 07306

Director: James Pustorino,
Exhibitions Director & Curator: Anne Trauben
visit our website: www.drawingrooms.org
©2020 Victory Hall Inc.

Drawing Rooms is a nonprofit art space and gallery in the Journal Square neighborhood in Jersey City. We show two and three-dimensional works by emerging and mid-career artists in NJ and the NY metropolitan area. Our innovative and exciting exhibitions, public programs and publications enrich the lives of our community through an appreciation of and involvement with contemporary art. Drawing Rooms is operated by Victory Hall Inc. a 501(c)(3) non-profit organization producing exhibitions, programs and public art projects in the NJ/NY area since 2001.

This program is made possible in part by funds from the New Jersey State Council on the Arts /Department of State, a partner agency of the National Endowment for the Arts, administered by the Hudson County Office of Cultural and Heritage Affairs, Thomas A. DeGise, County Executive, and the Board of Chosen Freeholders.